MAJOR LYRICISTS OF THE NORTHERN SUNG
A.D. 960–1126

BY JAMES J. Y. LIU

Major Lyricists of the
Northern Sung

A.D. 960-1126

**PRINCETON UNIVERSITY
PRESS**

Library of Congress Cataloging in Publication
Data will be found on the last printed page of this book.
This book has been composed in IBM Selectric Journal Roman

Printed in the United States of America
by Princeton University Press, Princeton, New Jersey

ACKNOWLEDGMENTS

I am grateful to the Committee on East Asian Studies and the Chinese-Japanese Language and Area Center, both of Stanford University, for research grants that made possible the writing of this book.

During the initial stage of my work I was assisted by Mrs. Rosa Kuei-ling Yang (née Wang), who performed such tedious but necessary tasks as compiling lists of meters used by each poet and of grammatical particles. I remain, however, solely responsible for all opinions expressed.

I am indebted to Professor Irving Yucheng Lo of Indiana University for having read the typescript and suggesting improvements, and to my student Mr. Kuo-ch'ing Tu for helping me read works in Japanese.

Finally, I wish to thank Professor Yen Yuan-shu, editor of the *Tamkang Review*, for permission to reprint material dealing with the lyrics of Liu Yung, which first appeared in that journal (Vol. 1, No. 2, Taipei, 1970) as an article and now forms part of Chapter 2; and also Professor Cyril Birch, editor of the volume *Studies in Chinese Literary Genres* (Berkeley, University of California Press, 1973) for permission to reprint several translations and commentaries.

J.J.Y.L.

Stanford, 1971

CONTENTS

MAJOR LYRICISTS OF THE NORTHERN SUNG
A.D. 960–1126

In this book, the word "lyric" is used as a translation of the Chinese word *tz'u*, which means "song-words."[1] As a generic term, it refers to the type of poetry originally written to existing tunes, usually in lines of unequal length (although this is not always the case), in contradistinction to certain other types of poetry known collectively as *shih* or "verse," which generally consist of lines of four, five, or seven syllables.

When and how the lyric originated are matters of scholarly controversy that we cannot go into here in detail. In any case, since a literary genre never comes into being overnight, it would be fruitless to try to pinpoint the beginning of the lyric to a precise date. Furthermore, if we consider any poetry intended for singing as an origin of the lyric, we shall have to trace its ancestry back to the earliest known Chinese poetry, that preserved in the *Book of Poetry (Shih-ching, ca.* 1100–550 B.C.), as has indeed been suggested.[2]   Another suggestion is that the lyric is derived from the Music Department songs (*yüeh-fu*) of the Han period (206 B.C. to A.D. 220), again because they were also intended for singing.[3] However, the songs in the *Book of Poetry* and the Music Department songs generally had their words written first, which were then set to music, whereas lyrics, in the vast majority of cases, were written to fit existing music. Apart from that, the *Book of Poetry* and the Music Department songs of the Han were too far removed in time from what is commonly recognized as

[1] Works are referred to by author, and when two or more works by the same author are used, a roman numeral is added, as in the bibliography. For abbreviations, see bibliography. In a previous work (J. J. Y. Liu, I, p. 30), I referred to the *tz'u* as "lyric meters." I now find this translation awkward when speaking of individual *tz'u* and have decided to use "lyrics" instead. However, I shall continue to use "lyric meters" when discussing the meters in which lyrics are written.

[2] See Lu K'an-ju and Feng Yüan-chün, p. 532; Ts'ai Te-an, pp. 12–13.

[3] Lu and Feng, *ibid.*; Liu Ta-chieh, *chung*, p. 155.

the lyric to be regarded as its origins. It seems more reasonable to see the inception of the lyric in the practice of some early sixth-century poets of writing songs in lines of unequal but fixed length to fit given tunes.[4] Such songs may be called the prototype of the lyric proper. Later, in the early eighth century, when folk poets and musicians wrote words to fit indigenous popular tunes or newly imported tunes from Central Asia, India, and possibly Southeast Asia (tunes that the traditional regular verses would not fit); or when they adapted regular verses for singing by such devices as the omission of certain syllables, the insertion of expletives, refrain, and melisma, then the lyric gradually emerged as a new poetic genre.[5] However, it was not until after the middle of the eighth century that a few famous poets began to write lyrics occasionally,[6] and not until the ninth century that the first important lyricist, Wen T'ing-yün (812–870?), appeared.

Thereafter, for over a century, the lyric continued to flourish, but it remained limited in scope and was still not considered as respectable as earlier types of poetry, at least in theory, although in fact even emperors and high ministers wrote lyrics. Then, during the eleventh century and the first quarter of the twelfth, the lyric at last attained its full florescence. This period corresponds roughly to what is known in political history as the Northern Sung dynasty (960–1126). Partly as a concession to convention and partly as a matter of convenience I am using the words "Northern Sung" in this book, although I am aware that as a general principle it is unsatisfactory to use a dynastic title as the designation of a period in literary history.[7]

Some scholars think that the peak of development of the lyric was reached during the subsequent Southern Sung period (1127–

---

[4]*Ibid.,* pp. 159–60.

[5]See Baxter, pp. 108–45 (pp. 186–255 in Bishop); Shih-ch'üan Ch'en, pp. 232–42.

[6]Some of the earliest lyrics by the literati were attributed to Li Po (701–762), and although the attribution has long been questioned, some recent writers have argued convincingly for his authorship. See Yang Hsien-yi, pp. 1–8; Chang Wan, pp. 19–24, 47–49, 93–98.

[7]See Wellek and Warren, pp. 262–63.

1279) rather than the Northern Sung. This is of course a matter of opinion. Anyway, even if we accept that a few Southern Sung lyricists may have surpassed their predecessors in some ways, it remains a fact that all of them, even the best, derived their respective styles from one Northern Sung lyricist or another. We may therefore still assert that the lyric attained full maturity and became a serious poetic genre during the Northern Sung, and it is to this period that we shall devote our attention.

Another question that we should consider briefly is the relative importance of Sung "verse" (*shih*) and Sung "lyrics" (*tz'u*). In the twentieth century, Chinese literary historians have tended to regard the lyric as the particular expression of the Sung literary genius while dismissing Sung verse as merely imitative of that of the T'ang period (618–907). This is no doubt a biased view, based on the questionable assumption that each historical period has its own special form of literary expression. On the other hand, to revert to the traditional attitude and say that the lyric is only a minor offshoot of the verse is surely going too far in the opposite direction.[8] Without denigrating Sung verse, we may fairly claim that the Sung lyric constitutes one of the chief glories of Chinese poetry.

This book is an attempt to examine critically the works of six representative poets who wrote in the lyric genre (not necessarily exclusively) during its heyday. I have chosen to discuss them in detail rather than to write a more comprehensive but inevitably more superficial survey of the history of the lyric during the Northern Sung period, because a long catalogue of poets and poems may produce a diffused if not confused impression. I hope that what losses this choice may entail may be compensated for by gains in depth and clarity. Naturally, the choice of "major" or "representative" poets of any age is in the last analysis a subjective one, influenced by the critic's preferences and prejudices. But a critic without prejudice is a critic without taste, and as long as the reader is aware of the critic's prejudices, he will be provoked into re-examining his own prejudices and

[8]See Yoshikawa, I, p. 9; II, p. 632.

assumptions and the critic will have performed a worthwhile task.

This being a critical study of poetry and not a cultural history or biography, I have concerned myself chiefly with the intrinsic qualities of the lyrics, and kept to a minimum historical and biographical information, which does not necessarily enhance our understanding or enjoyment of the lyrics.

The basic view of poetry adopted in this book is similar to that which I first sketched in *The Art of Chinese Poetry* (1962) and subsequently developed in "Towards a Chinese Theory of Poetry" (*Yearbook of Comparative and General Literature*, 1966, reprinted with minor revisions in *The Poetry of Li Shang-yin*, 1969). The critical standards applied, as well as the methods of analysis and the terminology, are also similar to what I have employed before, with some modifications. For readers not familiar with my previous works, I shall briefly describe my conception of poetry and explain my procedure and terminology.

Basically, I conceive of poetry as a double exploration of worlds and of language. By a "world" is meant a fusion of external reality and inner experience, and by "exploration of worlds" is meant the poet's probing of the natural world and the human world in which he lives, as well as his own mind. As for "exploration of language," this refers to the poet's incessant efforts to embody the worlds he explores in complex verbal structures and to realize the potentialities of the language in which he writes as a medium of poetic expression.[9] In the ensuing discussions on Northern Sung lyricists, their works will be analyzed and evaluated in terms of their explorations of worlds and of the Chinese language.

It should be pointed out that the "world" of a poem is not the same as its "theme," for the theme of a poem is something abstract and general, whereas its world is the concrete embodiment and individualization of a theme.

In the analysis of each poet's exploration of language, attention will be drawn to various elements of poetic style, such as diction,

[9]For more detailed discussions, see J. J. Y. Liu, I, pp. 91-100; II, pp. 199-206.

syntax, imagery, allusions, and prosody. Some of the terms I use may require clarification. With regard to imagery, I distinguish "simple images" from "compound images": the former are verbal expressions that evoke sensuous experiences without involving two objects; the latter may be subdivided into four types: compound images of juxtaposition (which place two objects side by side without any comparison), compound images of comparison (which compare one object, the "tenor," to another, the "vehicle"), compound images of substitution (which name the vehicle in lieu of the tenor), and compound images of transference (which transfer an attribute from an unidentified vehicle to the tenor).[10] Since compound images are poetically more important than simple ones, we shall pay more attention to the former. Among the four types of compound imagery, the first is so rare in Sung lyrics that it can be ignored. Thus, our discussions on imagery will focus on compound images of comparison, substitution, and transference, and the distinctions among these will become clear from examples.

I should further make clear that what I call "compound images of substitution" differ from other kinds of substitution that do not involve an underlying comparison of two things. In a compound image of substitution such as "green cloud" (which occurs in many lyrics as a substitute for a woman's hair), there is an implicit comparison of the tenor ("hair") to the vehicle ("cloud"), although only the latter is mentioned. By contrast, when "red" is used as a substitute for "flower" or "sail" as a substitute for "boat," no comparison is involved, only the substitution of an attribute for the object or of a part for the whole. In traditional Chinese criticism, all kinds of substitution are simply called "substitute words" (*tai tzu*). In traditional Western rhetoric, what I call "images of substitution" would be classified as metaphors, whereas the substitution of "red" for "flower" would be classified as metonymy, and that of "sail" for "boat" as synecdoche. I shall use the traditional Western terms for those substitutions which do not involve comparisons, but use the term

[10]Liu, I, pp. 101–09; II, pp. 236–40.

"images of substitution" rather than "metaphors" for those which do.

Earlier I mentioned "allusions" as an element of poetic style. Actually, there are several devices akin to allusions in Chinese poetry. First, an allusion proper occurs when a poet refers obliquely to history, legend, or earlier literature, and when the reader cannot understand the line in which the allusion occurs without recognizing what is being alluded to. Secondly, when a poet quotes a whole line or phrase verbatim from earlier literature, and when the present line makes sense even if the reader does not know its origin, but acquires a deeper significance if he does, then a "quotation" rather than an "allusion" is being used. Thirdly, when a poet uses expressions verbally similar to earlier writings, these can be called "derivations," which can be conscious borrowings or unconscious echoes. In either case, recognition of the source does not add to the meaning of the line, but only makes the reader realize the poet's familiarity with earlier writers and their influences on him. Derivations are therefore relevant to considerations of the poet's originality and his skill in using his sources, but irrelevant to an understanding of his works. Lastly, when a whole poem consists of lines adapted from earlier poetry or prose, it may be called an "adaptation," which requires some technical skill but can hardly be called creative writing. We shall have occasion to see examples of all these devices.[11]

Terms to be used in discussing prosody will be explained below, after I have first described how I shall proceed in the following chapters. For each lyricist, I shall first give a few of his works as examples, and then deal with his lyrics as a corpus. This procedure is followed for two purposes: to let the reader form a first impression of each poet's works before anything is said about his poetry in general, and to avoid constant interruptions of the discussions with distracting but necessary exegeses on individual poems. For each example given, the following will be provided:

1. The Chinese text, arranged in lines but without punctuation marks. (For line-divisions, see below.)

---

[11] For further discussions, see Liu, I, pp. 131–45.

2. Transliteration according to modern Pekinese pronunciation, with the rhyming syllables in reconstructed Ancient Chinese (which some scholars prefer to call Middle Chinese),[12] accompanied by a word-for-word translation.

3. A more idiomatic English translation, following the original line for line and reflecting the relative length of each line, with occasional uses of rhyme or assonance, but no attempt to reproduce the original rhyme scheme.

4. Exegetical notes when necessary.

5. A metrical diagram, details of which will be explained below.

6. A critical commentary.

For easy reference, the lyrics given as examples are numbered consecutively throughout the book.

As I mentioned at the outset, lyrics were originally written to musical tunes. Occasionally, a lyricist might compose his own tunes and write words to them, or write the words first and then set them to music,[13] but in most cases the tunes existed first. That is why each lyric bears a "tune-title" (tiao-ming). After the tunes were lost, the tune-titles became for all practical purposes names of meters. I have therefore referred to them simply as "meters" and have left them untranslated, only transliterated. Indeed, to have translated them might have been misleading. For example, to have given as the title of a lyric embodying historical consciousness and philosophical views the name "Nien-nu's Charms" (Nien-nu chiao, a tune originally named after a famous courtesan) would have been misleading or at least irrelevant.[14] However, when a lyricist adds a "sub-title" which is the real title of the poem, this has of course been translated.

[12] Ancient Chinese (or Middle Chinese) refers to Chinese of approximately A.D. 600–900. I have given the reconstructed A.C. pronunciations according to Karlgren, and when a character is not found in his Grammata Serica Recensa, I have reconstructed the pronunciation according to Ting Sheng-shu and then transcribed it into Karlgren's spelling, using the convenient table provided by Chou Fa-kao.

[13] Chiang K'uei said that he sometimes wrote the words first and then set them to music. See his preface to the lyric Ch'ang-t'ing-yüan man (CST, p. 2,181).

[14] See lyric No. 22 in this book.

We can now turn our attention to the prosody of lyric meters. Since the tunes used for Sung lyrics, with only a handful of exceptions,[15] have long been lost, we do not know how each metrical pattern was actually formed. Extant prosodic manuals of lyric meters (known as *tz'u-p'u*), which were all compiled after the music was lost, set forth standard patterns derived inductively from existing lyrics of the Sung and earlier periods. Thus, in a discussion of the prosody of a Sung lyric, it is sometimes hard to say how far the writer has deviated from the standard pattern, for the "standard pattern" may well have been based on this very lyric. However, when dealing with commonly used meters, we can see what the general practice was, and how an individual writer departed from it. When dealing with a lyric that is the earliest known example of a particular meter, we may observe interesting features that were presumably the innovations of the first writer.

The main prosodic features of lyric meters, and some of the problems encountered in discussing them, may be described under the following headings.

1. *Number and length of lines.* It is not always easy to divide a lyric into lines, for several reasons. First, in traditional editions, lyrics (like any other kind of writing in Chinese) are printed without any punctuation marks, all the words of one lyric being printed as one piece, with a blank space indicating the break between two stanzas, but no line-divisions. Secondly, the same Chinese word *chü* is used to denote either a syntactic unit ("sentence" in English) or a metrical unit ("line" in English). Hence, Chinese prosodists, in deciding what a "line" is, tend to be guided by the syntax and meaning rather than the rhythm. Likewise, modern editors of lyrics generally punctuate them according to the meaning, and some of the punctuation marks they add actually obscure the metrical pattern. Thirdly, there is no commonly used Chinese term corresponding to "enjambment" in Western prosody, although the phenomenon does exist in Chinese

[15] Seventeen tunes by Chiang K'uei are the only extant Sung *tz'u* music. For discussions and transcriptions, see Rulan Chao Pian, pp. 33–38, 99–130.

poetry, contrary to what has often been asserted. Some examples of enjambment can be found in T'ang verse,[16] and many more are seen in Sung lyrics. But Chinese prosodists are inclined to regard two metrical units that are syntactically inseparable as one "line." Finally, lyricists writing in the same meter do not necessarily follow the same syntactic pattern, so that it is not always clear where one "line" ends and another one begins. For example, a sequence of thirteen syllables may, syntactically speaking, consist of a pentasyllabic segment followed by an octosyllabic one, or vice versa.[17] Of course, ideally we should divide lyrics into lines purely on metrical grounds, without regard to syntax or meaning. Unfortunately we cannot do so, since we do not know the music that formed the basis of each meter. The original lyricists presumably knew how many syllables there should be to each beat of music, what the "tone pattern" (for which see below) should be to agree with the melodic line, where a rhyme should fall to coincide with the end of a musical phrase, and where a pause should be to accommodate a change of breath. Since we do not know any of these things, we have no other basis for deciding what a meter is than existing manuals, which, by their compilers' own admissions, divided lyrics into lines according to meaning.[18]

In this book I have arranged the Chinese text of each lyric in lines, after consulting various prosodic manuals and modern editions. I give as a separate line each metrical unit, whether it ends with a rhyme (marked in the manuals and some editions with the word *yün* or "rhyme") or without a rhyme (marked with the word *chü* or "line"). Where the rhythm seems to demand it, I also give as separate lines some metrical units regarded by prosodists as segments (marked with the word *tou* or "pause"). In this way I hope to show the interplay between the prescribed metrical rhythm and the actual syntactic rhythm. No punctuation marks are used, since they may obscure the metrical pattern.

Keeping in mind the difficulties of dividing a lyric into lines, we may nevertheless go on to speak of the length of lines. Generally,

---

[16]See J. J. Y. Liu, II, p. 230.
[17]Liang Ch'i-hsün, p. 35.
[18]Prefatory remarks *(fan-li)* in TL and TP.

lines vary from one to eleven syllables, but a line of eight or more syllables can often be considered a combination of two shorter lines.[19]

2. *Tone pattern.* Since the fifth century A.D., Chinese poets and prosodists have recognized four "tones" (*sheng*) in the language, called "Level" (*p'ing*), "Rising" (*shang*), "Falling" (or "Departing," *ch'ü*), and "Entering" (*ju*). These are not identical with the four tones of modern Pekinese, and the precise character of each tone in Ancient Chinese is a matter of conjecture.[20] However, the description of modern Pekinese tones as "contrasting contours of pitch, intensity, length, and glottolization"[21] can presumably apply to the four tones of Ancient Chinese as well. From the seventh century onwards, the four tones were classified into two main categories, "Level" and "Oblique" (or "Deflected," *tse,* which comprises the Rising, Falling, and Entering Tones), and it was the contrast and interplay between these two kinds of tones that formed the tone patterns of Regulated Verse (*lü-shih*).[22]   The broad distinction between Level and Oblique Tones continued to be observed in lyric meters, each of which has a fixed tone pattern, although some flexibility is allowed.   Lyricists who were familiar with the music or composed their own music would know when a syllable had to be of a certain tone and when it could be changed, according to its position in the melody.   Later writers, who did not know the music, copied their predecessors syllable for syllable and tone for tone,[23] or "filled in" (*t'ien*) the words according to the patterns set forth in the manuals.   As for prosodists, they can judge only by the extant works of early lyricists.   When, for a given syllable in a given meter, all extant specimens use the same tone, it is assumed

---

[19] Cf. Wang Li, p. 635.

[20] See Mei Tsu-lin, pp. 86–110.

[21] Fisher-Jorgensen, p. 219.   I am indebted to my colleague Professor Kung-yi Kao for this reference.

[22] Cf. J. J. Y. Liu, I, pp. 26–27; Downer and Graham, pp. 145–48; Jakobson, pp. 597–605.

[23] For example, Fang Ch'ien-li and Yang Tse-min copied the lyrics of Chou Pang-yen in this way. See Hsia Ch'eng t'ao, I, p. 76.

to be inflexible. When some lyricists use one tone but others use another, it is assumed to be flexible. In the metrical diagrams following the examples in this book, I have marked a Level Tone with the sign -, an Oblique Tone with the sign +, a Level that may be replaced by an Oblique with ∓, and the reverse with ±. Prosodic manuals differentiate only Level and Oblique Tones, though some Sung lyricists made further distinctions between two kinds of Level Tones, called *yin* or "Feminine" and *yang* or "Masculine," and among the three kinds of Oblique Tones. Since these finer tonal distinctions are not universally observed, I have not marked them in the diagrams but have mentioned them in discussing individual lyricists. The tone pattern given for each meter follows the Ancient Chinese pronunciation, and differs sometimes from the modern Pekinese pronunciation, which is given in the transliteration. I have therefore not included tone marks in the transliterations, to avoid discrepancies between these and the metrical diagrams. There are two reasons why I did not transliterate the whole text of each lyric according to the Ancient Chinese pronunciation: first, a transliteration using any one of the existing orthographic systems for reconstructed Ancient Chinese would be quite unpronounceable, whereas one using the Wade-Giles system for spelling modern Pekinese (the one used here) at least gives some idea of the sound of the words; secondly, most Chinese readers now read the lyrics in modern Pekinese pronunciation.

3. *Pauses.* In lyric meters, lines having the same number of syllables do not necessarily have a pause (or pauses) in the same position (or positions). For instance, a pentasyllabic line usually has a pause after the second syllable, forming a 2:3 rhythm, but it may have a pause after the third syllable, making the rhythm 3:2. It may even have a pause after the first syllable, in which case it may be considered a tetrasyllabic unit preceded by an initial monosyllabic segment, which is called in Chinese *yi-tzu-tou* or "one-word-pause."[24] Prosodic manuals do not mark pauses when they occur in what are considered normal positions (such as after the fourth syllable in a heptasyllabic line), but mark

[24]Wang Li, pp. 585-86; 634-37; Liang Ch'i-hsün, pp. 44, 46.

them when they occur in "abnormal" positions (such as after the third syllable in a heptasyllabic line).   Since the Western reader cannot be assumed to know where a pause is normally expected to be, I have marked each pause with a stroke (/) in the diagrams, whether it is marked *tou* or not in the manuals and modern editions.   In fact, sometimes there is no universal agreement where a pause should be marked, and whether a given syllable should be considered the unrhymed ending of a line (*chü*), or the end of a segment followed by a pause (*tou*).[25]   When individual writers introduce additional pauses or shift the positions of pauses, I have not marked these in the diagrams but have pointed them out in the discussions.   Incidentally, in view of the complexities just mentioned, it seems best not to use the word "caesura" in talking about pauses in Chinese lyric meters.

4. *Rhyme*. Some lyric meters use one rhyme throughout; others use two or more rhymes.   Both Level-toned and Oblique-toned syllables can be used as rhymes, but not interchangeably, the tone pattern of each meter being fixed.   In other words, whether a rhyming syllable should have a Level Tone or an Oblique Tone depends on its position in the meter.   In the metrical diagrams in this book, I have marked Level-toned rhymes with capital letters and Oblique-toned rhymes with small letters. For example, *A* and *B* represent two rhymes, both Level-toned; *A* and *b* represent, respectively, a Level-toned rhyme and an Oblique-toned one; *A* and *a* represent syllables having the same finals (and sometimes the same initials as well) but different tones.

The two kinds of Level Tones, Feminine and Masculine, are generally interchangeable as rhymes.   Syllables in the Rising and Falling Tones are used interchangeably as rhymes, but those in the Entering Tone are kept separate.[26]

Internal rhymes are recognized by some scholars, who call them "rhymes-within-the-line" (*chü-chung-yün*)[27] or "hidden rhymes" (*an-yün*).[28]   However, since there is no universal agree-

25 Wang Li, pp. 650–51.
26 Hsia Ch'eng-t'ao, I, pp. 22–52.
27 *Ibid.*, pp. 32–35.
28 Liang Ch'i-hsün, pp. 54–55.

ment about the division of lines, what is an internal rhyme to some can be regarded as an end-rhyme by others who take the syllables following the rhyme as another line. I have chosen the latter alternative, for the simple reason that it is easier to mark an end-rhyme than an internal one. The rhymes used in lyric meters have been grouped into nineteen categories.[29] Of these, fourteen are subdivided into Level, Rising, and Falling Tones, and five consist of syllables in the Entering Tone only. Because Rising and Falling Tones can be used interchangeably, they may be considered one sub-division. Thus, in fact, there are altogether thirty-three categories of rhymes in lyric meters:

> Categories I-XIV: 14 in Level Tones
>   14 in Rising and Falling Tones
> Categories XV-XIX: 5 in the Entering Tone

These categories were established by post-Sung prosodists, based on the actual practice of Sung lyricists, and were not prescribed in Sung times. The Sung poets apparently rhymed according to their own pronunciations when writing lyrics,[30] although they usually followed the standard T'ang rhyme categories when writing Regulated Verse. Since reconstructions of Ancient Chinese by modern phonologists are ultimately based on the rhyme dictionary Ch'ieh-yün by Lu Fa-yen completed in A.D. 601, they naturally cannot accurately reflect eleventh-century or twelfth-century pronunciation. But since we do not have anything closer to Sung pronunciation, we still have to borrow the reconstructed T'ang pronunciations as approximations, on the understanding that some phonological differences shown in the orthography may have disappeared in Sung pronunciation. For instance, the finals ung, uong, iung, and iwong were all used as rhymes by Sung lyricists, which suggests that these syllables, originally pronounced differently, had become indistinguishable by Sung times. My reason for including the reconstructed pronunciations of rhyming syllables is simply to indicate the

---

[29] Wang Li, pp. 534–82.
[30] Hsia Ch'eng-t'ao, I, p. 51.

rhyme scheme of each lyric, not to show how these syllables should actually be pronounced.

Finally, I should like to say that in the translations of the lyrics I have tried to preserve some of the characteristic conciseness and polysemy (or "ambiguity" in the Empsonian sense) of Chinese poetry, without doing violence to English grammar and idiom. In particular, although in Chinese poetry the subject of a verb is often unidentified, I have sometimes added pronouns as subjects, partly because not to do so might result in pidgin English and partly because in a lyric there is generally a distinct poetic or dramatic *persona* as the "speaker" of the poem, unlike some Chinese nature poems of an impersonal character, which may be spoiled by the introduction of personal pronouns. Similarly, I have often added connective particles where none is used in the original, for the omission of such particles is a common linguistic feature in Chinese, but in English it becomes a self-conscious rhetorical device known as asyndeton, which, if used too often, may turn into an irritating mannerism and also break up the rhythm. As for the concrete imagery for which Chinese poetry is justly famous, and such structural features as parallelism, antithesis, repetition, and enjambment, I trust I have kept them intact in my translations.

CHAPTER 1

Sentiment and Sensibility

Yen Shu (991-1055) and Ou-yang Hsiu (1007-1072)

Most poets of the early Sung regarded the lyric as a poetic genre suitable for only a limited range of themes and emotions. They used it to express sentimental love or groundless ennui, to describe beautiful women or pleasant scenery, to capture nostalgic moods or enchanted moments; but when it came to more public themes or more serious thoughts, they would write in the *shih* form. In this they were but following an earlier tradition, the tradition of the lyricists of the Hua-chien School (named after the anthology *Hua-chien chi* or "Among the Flowers," which covers the period 836–940), although the great lyric poet Li Yü (better known as Li Hou-chu or "Li the Last Ruler," 937–978) had already departed from this tradition to some extent when he wrote lyrics to give vent to his anguish and despair after the loss of his kingdom, the Southern T'ang. The early Sung lyricists were for the most part content to revert to the familiar themes of the Hua-chien poets, but they treated these themes with greater depth and subtlety, and also explored the verbal potentials of the lyric as a poetic medium further than their predecessors did. In so far as they cultivated refined feelings and sensibilities, they may be called "sentimentalists," not in the modern pejorative sense, but rather in the eighteenth-century sense of the word. Among these lyric poets, Yen Shu and Ou-yang Hsiu are outstanding representatives.

These two men had much in common: both were natives of what is now Kiangsi province, both came from relatively poor families but rose to the highest offices in government, and both were known as upright and outspoken Confucian scholar-officials.[1] Yet both wrote lyrics that betray hardly any trace of

[1] For Yen Shu's biography, see Wan Min-hao, *passim,* and Hsia Ch'eng-t'ao, III, pp. 197–270; for Ou-yang Hsiu's, see J. T. C. Liu, *passim.*

their Confucian public images but reveal something of their individual modes of sensibility, as the following examples of their works will show.

No. 1   Yen Shu

晏　殊

浣溪沙

一曲新詞酒一杯
去年天氣舊亭台
夕陽西下幾時迴

無可奈何花落去
似曾相識燕歸來
小園香徑獨徘徊

Huan Hsi Sha

yi   ch'ü   hsin   tz'u   chiu   yi   pei   (puâi)
one   tune   new   word   wine   one   cup

ch'ü-nien   t'ien-ch'i   chiu   t'ing   t'ai   (d'âi)
last-year   weather   old   pavilion   tower

hsi-yang   hsi   hsia   chi-shih   hui   (γ uai)
evening-sun   west   set   what-time   return

wu-k'o-nai-ho   hua   lo-ch'ü
nothing-to-be-done   flower   fall-away

ssu-ts'eng-hsiang-shih   yen   kuei-lai   (lâi)
seem-to-have-known   swallow   come-back

hsiao   yüan   hsiang   ching   tu   p'ai-huai   (γ uâi)[2]
little   garden   fragrant   path   alone   pace-to-and-fro

[2]CST, p. 89. For easy reference, all texts of lyrics are taken from the CST. When a variant reading from another edition is adopted, the fact will be noted.

A song with newly written words; of wine, a cup.
Last year's weather, the same pavilions and towers.
The sun is setting in the west: when will it return?

Nothing to be done about the flowers' falling away.
Seeming acquaintances—the swallows coming back.
A little garden, a fragrant path; alone pacing to and fro.

Meter[3]

```
±  +  -  -  /  ±  +  -  A
±  -  ∓  +  /  +  -  -  A
∓  -  ±  +  /  +  -  -  A

∓  +  ±  -  /  -  +  +  0
±  -  ∓  +  /  +  -  -  A
±  -  ∓  +  /  +  -  -  A
```

Commentary

This lyric reveals a confined and intimate world, in which Nature is seen in its more familiar aspects only, as if it were a garden, revealing little of what lies beyond its walls. The emotions implied are delicate rather than intense, and the sensibility revealed is highly refined. The verbal structure that embodies this exclusive world is correspondingly subtle and exquisite, despite its apparent simplicity.

The first two lines describe pleasant surroundings that, one would have thought, might have induced a gay and happy mood in the speaker, but on further reading one realizes this is not so. The reason is suggested by a paradox that underlies the situation: everything *seems* to be the same as before, but actually a year has passed, so that nothing is really the same. This underlying paradox is made a little more explicit in the next line, where the seemingly childish question "when will it return?" emphasizes the irretrievable passage of time, for although one knows that the sun will rise again tomorrow, will it be the same sun as today's? Pursuing this Heraclitean idea, one may ask if spring will come back, and if one's youth will ever come back. Such questions, although not overtly asked by the poet, are implicit in the first line of the second stanza, where the falling of the flowers suggests

[3]Cf. TL, 3, p. 14b; TP, 4, p. 18b; TF, 5 *hsia*, p. 71.

the passing away of spring and of youth, while the speaker's feeling of helplessness in the face of the relentless rush of time is expressed by the phrase "nothing to be done" (*wu-k'o-nai-ho*). However, the next line raises a glint of hope by suggesting that the same swallows as last year's are coming back. Thus, these two lines, which in the original form an exact antithesis (an antithesis demanded by the meter), do much more than match words precisely in sense and in tone; they reveal two conflicting emotional attitudes—whereas the first line shows regret and sadness at the transciency of life symbolized by the falling flowers, the next line offers some consolation by creating at least an illusion of permanency, since the returning swallows form a link with the past. No wonder, then, that this couplet has been much admired, not least by Yen Shu himself, who liked it so much that he also used it in a poem in Regulated Verse.[4] The unresolved emotional tension is retained in the last line, where the image of pacing to and fro, evoked by the rhyming disyllable *p'ai-huai* (Ancient Chinese *b'uai-γuai*), together with the reiterative sound of the syllables themselves, perfectly embodies the speaker's vacillating state of mind.

No. 2

鵲踏枝
(蝶戀花)

檻菊愁烟蘭泣露
羅幕輕寒
燕子雙飛去
明月不諳離恨苦
斜光到曉穿朱戶

4 T'ang Kuei-chang, IV, p. 12.

昨夜西風凋碧樹
獨上高樓
望盡天涯路
欲寄采箋兼尺素
山長水闊知何處

Ch'üeh T'a Chih
(also called *Tieh Lüan Hua*)

chien	chü			ch'ou	yen	lan		ch'i	lu	(luo)
fence	chrysanthemum			grieve	mist	orchid		weep	dew	

lo   mu   ch'ing han
silk curtain light cold

yen-tzu shuang fei-ch'ü   (k'iwo)
swallow pair   fly-away

ming	yüeh	pu	an	li	hen	k'u	(k'uo)
bright	moon	not	acquainted	parting	sorrow	bitter	

hsia	kuang	tao-hsiao	ch'uan	chu	hu	(ɤuo)
slant	light	till-dawn	pierce	vermilion	door	

tso-yeh	hsi-feng	tiao	pi	shu	(ziu)
last-night	west-wind	wither	green	tree	

tu   shang kao lou
alone mount tall tower

wang chin   t'ien-ya   lu (luo)
gaze exhaustively heaven-end road

yü	chi	ts'ai-chien	chien	ch'ih-su	(suo)
wish	send	colored-paper	and	foot-long white-silk	

shan	ch'ang	shui	k'uo	chih	ho-ch'u	(ts'iwo)[5]
mountain	long	water	broad	know	what-place	

[5]CST, p. 91.

Chrysanthemums by the fence grieve at the mist,
orchids weep dew.
   The silk curtain is slightly cold,
   And swallows fly away in pairs.
The bright moon, not acquainted with the bitterness of
parting sorrow,
Continues to pierce the vermilion door with its slant
beams till dawn.

Last night the west wind withered the green trees.
   Alone I mounted the lofty tower
   To gaze at the roads, as far as the
   world's end.
I wish to send letters on colored paper and white silk,
But beyond distant mountains and broad streams, who knows
where?

Meter[6]

```
±  +  ∓  -  /  -  +  +  a
      ∓  +  -  -  0
      ±  +  /  -  -  +  a
∓  +  ±  -  /  -  +  +  a
∓  -  ±  +  /  -  -  +  a

±  +  ∓  -  /  -  +  +  a
      ∓  +  -  -  0
      ±  +  /  -  -  +  a
∓  +  ±  -  /  -  +  +  a
∓  -  ±  +  /  -  -  +  a
```

In this lyric Yen Shu uses the finals *uo, iwo,* and *iu* as rhymes, a common practice among lyricists. The rhymes at the ends of lines 4 and 5 belong to the Rising Tone, while all the other rhyming syllables belong to the Falling Tone. (The word *hu,* "door," which is now pronounced in the Falling Tone, was pronounced in the Rising Tone.)

[6]Cf. TL, 8, p. 6b; TP, 13, p. 13a; TF, 8 *shang,* p. 55.

Commentary

The emotional element in this lyric is stronger than in No. 1, as can be seen from the choice of such words as *ch'ou* ("grieve"), *ch'i* ("weep"), *han* ("cold"), *k'u* ("bitter"), and *tiao* ("wither"). The imagery is drawn from Nature, which is seen under the Pathetic Fallacy in some respects but as indifferent or even hostile to human beings in other respects: the chrysanthemums and orchids are imagined to share human emotions, and the swallows also seem to be sensitive to the emotional atmosphere as well as the physical environment, but the moon and the wind are shown as indifferent to human suffering and even adding to the forlorn atmosphere. In stanza 2, line 3 involves some ambiguity: the words *wang chin t'ien-ya lu* can be construed as meaning, "to gaze at *all* the roads that lead to the end of the world," or "to gaze *as far as possible,* at the roads that lead to the end of the world," but either way the line expresses yearning for the absent one. In line 4, the use of "foot-long white silk" for a letter is a conventional expression and need not be considered an allusion.

No. 3

清平樂

金風細細
葉葉梧桐墜
綠酒初嘗人易醉
一枕小窗濃睡

紫薇朱槿花殘
斜陽却照闌干
雙燕欲歸時節
銀屏昨夜微寒

Ch'ing P'ing Yüeh

chin	feng	hsi-hsi	(siei)
metal	wind	small-small	

yeh-yeh	wu-t'ung	chui	(â'wi)
leaf-leaf	wu-t'ung	fall	

lu	chiu	ch'u	ch'ang	jen	yi	tsui	(tswi)
green	wine	first	taste	person	easy	drunk	

yi	chen	hsiao	ch'uang	nung	shui	(źwie)
one	pillow	small	window	thick	sleep	

tzu-wei	chu-chin	hua	ts'an	(dz'ân)
crape-myrtle	red-hibiscus	flower	fade	

hsia	yang	ch'üeh	chao	lan-kan	(kân)
slant	sun	still	shine	railing	

shuang	yen	yü	kuei	shih-chieh
pair	swallow	wish	return	time-season

yin	p'ing	tso-yeh	wei	han	(γan)[7]
silver	screen	last-night	slight	cold	

The autumn wind is soft, so soft—
One by one, *wu-t'ung* leaves fall.
A first taste of the green wine easily makes one drunk;
On a pillow by the small window, a deep slumber.

The crape-myrtle and the red hibiscus wither away,
But the slanting sun still shines on the balustrade.
It is time for the pair of swallows to go home:
Last night, the silver screen was slightly cold.

Note

St. 1, l. 1. Autumn wind. *Chin-feng,* literally "metal wind," a conventional expression for "autumn wind," since autumn was

[7]CST, p. 92.

supposed to correspond to metal, one of the "five elements" (*wu-hsing*).

Meter[8]

```
        ±  ∓  ±  +  a
        ±  +  /  -  -  +  a
   ±  +  ∓  -  /  -  ∓  +  a
   ∓  +  /  ∓  -  /  ∓  +  a

        ±  ±  /  ±  +  /  -  -  B
        ±  ∓  /  ±  +  /  ∓  -  B
        ±  +  /  ∓  -  /  ±  +  0
        ∓  ∓  /  ∓  +  /  -  -  B
```

All the rhyming syllables in the first stanza have the Falling Tone, those in the second stanza the Level Tone.

Commentary

A fusion of an autumn scene and its corresponding mood, this lyric is permeated with soft colors, mellow lights, and subdued emotions.   Nothing is overemphasized: the wind is "soft" (literally "small-small"); the leaves fall "one by one," not all at once; the wine is barely "tasted," not quaffed; the window is "small;" the screen "slightly" cold.   There is just a hint of sadness at the impending departure of the swallows, but no strong pro-testation of grief.   The diction is simple and elegant, with a few conventional phrases (*chin feng* or "metal wind" for "autumn wind," and *lu chiu* or "green wine"), but no allusions.   The imagery too is simple, relying for its effect on coherence rather than striking originality.   The reduplicative disyllables *hsi-hsi* (*siei-siei*) and *yeh-yeh* (*iäp-iäp*) suggest, respectively, the whistling of the wind and the sound of leaves falling, thus enhancing the effect of the imagery.

[8]Cf. CL, 4, p. 16b; TP, 15, p. 22b; TF, 6 *shang*, p. 13.

No. 4

踏莎行

小徑紅稀
芳郊綠遍
高台樹色陰陰見
春風不解禁楊花
濛濛亂撲行人面

翠葉藏鶯
朱簾隔燕
罏香靜逐游絲轉
一場愁夢酒醒時
斜陽却照深深院

T'a So Hsing

hsiao   ching   hung   hsi
little   path   red   scarce

fang   chiao   lu   pien   (pien)
fragrant   suburb   green   all-over

kao   t'ai   shu   se   yin-yin   hsien   (γien)
tall   tower   tree   color   shady-shady   appear

ch'un   feng   pu   chieh   chin   yang-hua
spring   wind   not   understand   forbid   willow-catkin

meng-meng   luan   p'u   hsing-jen   mien   (miän)
misty   disorder   dab   walking-man   face

ts'ui   yeh   ts'ang   ying
green-jade   leaf   hide   oriole

chu   lien   ke   yen   (.ien)
vermilion   curtain   separate   swallow

lu   hsiang   ching   chu   yu-ssu   chuan   (tîwän)
censer   incense   quiet   chase   gossamer   turn

yi-ch'ang   ch'ou   meng   chiu   hsing   shih
once   sorrow   dream   wine   wake   time

hsia   yang   ch'üeh   chao   shen-shen   yüan   (jiwän)[9]
slant   sun   still   shine   deep-deep   courtyard

Little path dotted with red,
Fragrant country covered with green.
By the lofty tower the trees spread their dark, dark
shades.
The spring wind knows not how to forbid the willow catkins,
All fuzzy and fluffy, to dab a walker's face at random.

Emerald leaves hide the orioles;
Vermilion curtains bar the swallows.
The incense smoke quietly follows the gossamers
drifting around.
At the moment of awakening from a sorrowful dream induced
by wine,
The slanting sun is still shining on the deep, deep
courtyard.

Meter[10]

```
          ±  +  -  -  0
          ∓  -  ±  +  a
∓  -  ±  +  /  -  -  +  a
±  -  ∓  +  /  +  -  -  0
∓  -  ±  +  /  -  -  +  a

          ±  +  -  -  0
          ∓  -  ±  +  a
∓  -  ±  +  /  -  -  +  a
∓  -  ±  +  /  +  -  -  0
∓  -  ±  +  /  -  -  +  a
```

[9]CST, p. 99.
[10]Cf. TL, 8, p. 18a; TP, 13, p. 3a; TF, 7 *hsia*, p. 53.

The two stanzas are identical in tone pattern and rhyme scheme. In this meter, it is common practice to use Oblique Tones as rhymes. Yen Shu has not only done so, but has also gone further by using only syllables in the Falling Tone as rhymes. The use of *ien* and *iän* as rhymes is acceptable in lyric meters.

Commentary

We need not follow those commentators who take this lyric as a political allegory,[11] but just examine how its world of groundless melancholy is embodied in its verbal structure.

The first two lines, with the help of metonymy ("red" for "flowers" and "green" for "grass"), not only paint a highly colorful scene but also hint at the passing of spring, for only a few fallen red petals remain on the path, while the countryside is overgrown with lush green grass. This impression is further deepened by the third line, which describes the thick foliage that has had time to grow on the trees. As the speaker walks along, he is annoyed by the floating willow catkins that keep striking gently against his face, like persistent melancholic feelings that refuse to be brushed aside. He then indulges in the poetic fancy that it is the spring wind that is to blame for not knowing how to forbid the catkins to irritate him.

In the second stanza, the scene gradually shifts to the interior. We first observe the green leaves outside the window, then the curtains that exclude the outside world, and finally the intimate atmosphere inside the room. The contrast between "emerald" and "vermilion" in the first two lines of this stanza echoes the similar contrast between "red" and "green" in the opening lines of the first stanza, and these contrasts are accompanied by tonal contrasts in the meter. We may also see a parallelism between the willow catkins in the first stanza and the incense smoke in the second, for both seem to symbolize elusive feelings of listlessness and melancholy. At the same time, the drifting incense smoke also suggests the extreme stillness of the air and the privacy of the room. Consequently the world of this lyric is felt to be private

[11] See Chang Hui-yen, p. 6b; T'ang Kuei-chang, IV, p. 16; Chiang Shang-hsien, II, p. 106.

and exclusive, embodying a cultured consciousness and reflecting a leisurely and aristocratic milieu. The examples quoted above are typical of the majority of Yen Shu's lyrics, which generally embody private and secluded worlds. The external environment they reflect is urbane and cultured; the inner experiences they explore are fragile and elusive. The mood may vary from gentle melancholy to mild enjoyment, but seldom do we encounter intense passion. The poet lingers over, dwells on, and savors his emotions, rather than getting them off his chest in outbursts. There is a feeling of stillness in his lyrics, as if everything were magically transfixed forever, like those figures on the Grecian urn in Keats's famous ode. Paradoxically, it is just because Yen Shu is so sensitive to time that he manages to arrest its flow, if only for a moment, in his songs, so that every precious detail, be it an external object or an inner experience, may be held up for contemplation. Such contemplation, however, is intuitive rather than intellectual. Yen does not express philosophic views in his lyrics, as do some later lyricists, but contents himself with probing and embodying refined sentiments and sophisticated modes of consciousness.

In style, Yen Shu's lyrics are graceful without being effeminate, and elegant without being affected or pedantic. The diction is refined for the most part, with occasional touches of colloquialism, but hardly ever slangy. In all his one hundred and thirty-six lyrics, I have noticed only some thirty expressions that may be considered "colloquial" and none that can justifiably be called "slang," although of course we cannot draw very precise distinctions between what is "colloquial" and what is "slang." On the other hand, there are very few allusions. The few allusions that do occur, such as those to P'an Yüeh as a handsome young man and to the "Peach-blossom Fountain" as fairyland,[12] are so common as to be idioms without particular poetic significance.

Syntactically, these lyrics generally do not differ very much from Classical Chinese prose. Naturally some lines do not contain verbs, such as the opening lines of lyrics No. 1 and No. 3.

[12]CST, pp. 92, 97.

Most lines are end-stopped, although there are a few instances of enjambment, such as:

君 莫 笑
醉 鄉 人
熙 熙 長 似 春

chün	*mo*	*hsiao*
you (sir)	don't	laugh

tsui-hsiang	*jen*
drunk-country	man

hsi-hsi	*ch'ang*	*ssu*	*ch'un*[13]
happy	always	like	spring

Do not laugh, sir,
At one in the land of intoxication,
Forever happy, as if it were eternal spring!

何 人 解 繫 天 邊 日
占 取 春 風
免 使 繁 紅
一 片 西 飛 一 片 東

ho-jen	*chieh*	*hsi*	*t'ien-pien*	*jih*
what-man	know-how	tie	heaven-side	sun

chan-ch'ü	*ch'un-feng*
occupy (suffix)	spring-wind

mien	*shih*	*fan*	*hung*
avoid	let	numerous	red

yi-p'ien	*hsi*	*fei*	*yi-p'ien*	*tung*[14]
one-petal	west	fly	one-petal	east

[13] *Ibid.,* p. 90.
[14] *Ibid.,* p. 93.

Who could tie up the sun over the horizon
And control the spring wind
So that the numerous red petals
Would not fly, one to the east, one to the west?

The presence of enjambment adds to the fluency of the rhythm. In versification, Yen shows considerable care and ingenuity. As we have noted above, he sometimes uses only syllables in the Falling Tone as rhymes, though this is not obligatory. Even for syllables that are not rhymes, as Hsia Ch'eng-t'ao has pointed out, Yen Shu often pays special attention to the Falling Tone: if he uses a Falling Tone for a certain syllable in one stanza, he would match it with another Falling Tone in the corresponding position in the second stanza.[15] For example, in the meter *Ts'ai Sang Tzu,* the tone pattern of the last line of each of the two stanzas is:

$$+ \ + \ - \ - \ / \ + \ + \ -$$

In Yen's lyrics written in this meter, with one single exception, the penultimate syllable is a Falling Tone in both stanzas.[16] Such attention to details of versification suggests that Yen was not only concerned with the purely literary qualities of his lyrics but also with the musical qualities of his words. Now, although we no longer have the music to which his lyrics were written, we can still perceive their carefully wrought tone patterns.

Yen's lyrics do not involve a great number of meters. Altogether thirty-eight meters are used, of which thirty-four are "little airs" (*hsiao-ling,* i.e., containing sixty-two or fewer syllables), and only four are "slow lyrics" (*man-tz'u,* i.e., containing sixty-three or more syllables).[17] The longest of the meters used consists of eighty-two syllables, the shortest of forty.[18] All are in two stanzas. These short meters do not afford much scope for extended description, but are well suited to Yen's artistic pur-

---

[15]Hsia Ch'eng-t'ao, I, pp. 56–58.
[16]CST, pp. 92–93.
[17]The criterion adopted here for differentiating *hsiao-ling* and *man-tz'u* is that proposed by Wang Li (p. 520).
[18]The longest meter is *Fu Ni-shang,* the shortest *Chiu-ch'üan Tzu.*

pose: to capture exquisite moments and changing moods. Nineteen of the meters are not known to have been used by anyone before him; in other words, he was the first to write words to the tunes that gave rise to these meters.

Imagery abounds in Yen Shu's lyrics. Many of the images are drawn from Nature, especially its gentler manifestations: flowers, trees, birds, mists, and hills. Others are drawn from everyday life: pavilions, courtyards, curtains, screens, and so forth. These kinds of imagery naturally contribute to the delicate and intimate atmosphere of his lyrics. In form Yen's images include both simple and compound ones. Examples of simple imagery can easily be found in the lyrics quoted above. Compound imagery is more interesting and deserves more detailed discussion.

Compound images involving comparison and those involving substitution both occur frequently. Sometimes human features are compared to natural objects, such as in

> Her hair, drooping over her temples, seems
> about to meet the new moon on her eyebrows;

> The red flush, caused by wine, has just
> appeared on her face—sunset clouds![19]

Although these images are not original, they gain some force by their coherence in visual appeal and emotional associations. In one lyric, human life itself is compared to natural objects:

> How much longer is it than a spring dream?
> And when it disperses, it is like autumn clouds,
> nowhere to be found.[20]

Again, these images are not original; indeed, the two lines are taken practically verbatim from a lyric by Po Chü-yi,[21] where they apparently describe a mysterious love affair. By applying them to life itself, Yen Shu gives them a new significance.

Sometimes the process of comparison is reversed: natural objects are likened to human beings or man-made objects. In one lyric, Yen Shu writes,

[19] CST, p. 90. See also p. 94.
[20] Ibid., p. 95.
[21] Po Chü-yi, 12, p. 12a.

> [The east wind] has suddenly opened the
willow's green moth-eyebrows

> And secretly split the crab-apple's pink
powdered face.[22]

In another one, he compares the new moon to eyebrows knit in sorrow, and falling flowers to tears dropping.[23] The effect of such images can be merely pretty, as in the examples just given, but it can also be strongly emotive, as in

> Autumn dew falls
> And sheds all the Southern orchid's red tears.[24]

This is one of Yen's favorite images, one that he uses in several other lyrics, including No. 2, quoted before.

The best images, it seems to me, are those which fuse Nature and human emotion in such a way as to make it difficult or impossible for us to say which is the tenor and which the vehicle of the compound image in each case. Consider, for instance, this line describing willows:

> The rainy twigs and misty leaves tie
up one's feelings.[25]

Or these lines describing a love tryst:

> Let this love be
> A thousand-foot gossamer
> To induce the morning cloud to stay![26]

In each of these images, the emotion finds a perfect correlative in the natural object, and it is of no importance to decide which is being compared to which.

By contrast, images of substitution often degenerate into clichés, like "green hills" for "eyebrows," "autumn waves" for "eyes," "cherries" for "lips," and "spring onions" for "fingers."[27]

[22]CST, p. 95.
[23]Ibid., p. 96.
[24]Ibid., p. 96.
[25]Ibid., p. 90.
[26]Ibid., p. 97.
[27]Ibid., pp. 90, 95, 96.

All these hackneyed images add little to the poetic effect.

Some images, such as the falling flowers in No. 1, the catkins and incense smoke in No. 4, and the spring dream and autumn clouds mentioned before, are not merely descriptions of particular objects but representations of universal experiences or concepts, and may therefore be considered symbols, one of the chief distinctive features of which is the universality of significance.

To sum up: most of Yen Shu's lyrics embody worlds of sentiment and sensibility in verbal structures that are delicate and subtle. However, he also wrote some lyrics eulogizing the emperor or congratulating himself on his birthday, in a language trite and conventional. These lyrics can best be described as social embellishment or light entertainment, and need not be taken into serious consideration in an assessment of his total achievement as a lyricist.

No. 5   Ou-yang Hsiu

歐陽修
踏莎行

雨霽風光
春分天氣
千花百卉爭明媚
畫梁新燕一雙雙
玉籠鸚鵡愁孤睡

薜荔依牆
莓苔滿地
青樓幾處歌聲麗
蕭然舊事上心來
無言斂皺眉山翠

T'a So Hsing

yü-chi   feng-kuang
clear-after-rain view

ch'un-fen   t'ien-ch'i   (k'jẹi)
vernal-equinox   weather

ch'ien   hua   po   hui   cheng ming-mei   (mji)
thousand flower hundred plant vie   bright-charm

hua   liang hsin yen   yi-shuang-shuang
painted beam   new   swallow one-pair-pair

yü   lung ying-wu ch'ou ku   shui   (żwiẹ)
jade cage parrot   grieve alone sleep

pi-li   yi   ch'iang
creeper cling wall

mei-t'ai man   ti   (d'i)
lichen   fill ground

ch'ing-lou   chi-ch'u   ko-sheng   li   (liei)
green-mansion several-place song-sound beautiful

mo-jan   chiu-shih shang hsin   lai
suddenly old-thing rise   heart (suffix)

wu-yen   lien-chou   mei-shan   ts'ui   (ts'wi)²⁸
no-word fold-wrinkle eyebrow-hill green

A clear view after rain;
   The weather, that of early spring:
Hundreds and thousands of flowers vie in bright-
   colored beauty.
On the painted beams, pairs of swallows have newly arrived.
In the jewelled cage, the parrot grieves to sleep alone.

   Creepers clinging to the wall,
   Lichen all over the ground—
From several Green Mansions comes the rich noise of songs.
Suddenly, memories of the past rise in her heart;
In silence she knits her eyebrows, dark as green hills.

²⁸ Ibid., p. 123.

Note

St. 2, l. 1. Creeper. *Pi-li,* or *Ficus pumilia,* a kind of creeper.
St. 2, l. 3. Green Mansions. *Ch'ing-lou,* conventional euphemism for houses of pleasure.

Meter

See No. 4 above.

Commentary

The lyric expresses the feelings of a neglected woman, as imagined by the poet. The beautiful view forms an ironic contrast with her solitude—a contrast made more noticeable by the further contrast between the happy pairs of swallows and the lonely parrot in the cage. Moreover, the parrot resembles the heroine in another way too: it is confined to a jewelled cage because of its ability to talk, just as she is confined to a luxurious harem because of her beauty and talent.

In the second stanza, the creepers and the lichen produce a gloomy, desolate atmosphere. Then, in line 3, the mention of Green Mansions strongly suggests that the heroine herself used to be a singing girl, and that now the sound of the carefree singing of the other girls reminds her of her past gay life. In the last line, the poet forms an effective image by combining two conventional expressions, *yüan-shan mei* or "distant-hill [-like] eyebrows," a phrase first applied to the famous beauty Chuo Wen-chün, and *ts'ui-mei* or "green eyebrows," a phrase used to describe the fashion, once popular among palace ladies, of painting the eyebrows a greenish color.

No. 6

生查子

去年元夜時
花市燈如晝
月到柳梢頭
人約黃昏後

今年元夜時
月與燈依舊
不見去年人
淚滿春衫袖

Sheng Cha Tzu[29]

ch'ü-nien   yüan-yeh   shih
last-year   prime-night   time

hua-shih   teng   ju   chou   (tiəu)
flower-market   lantern   like   daylight

yüeh   tao   liu   shao-t'ou
moon   reach   willow   tip-top

jen   yüeh   huang-hun   hou   (γəu)
man   date   twilight   after

chin-nien   yüan-yeh   shih
this-year   prime-night   time

yüeh   yü   teng   yi-chiu   (g'iəu)
moon   and   lantern   still-same

pu   chien   ch'ü-nien   jen
not   see   last-year   man

lei   man   ch'un   shan   hsiu   (ziəu)[30]
tear   fill   spring   gown   sleeve.

Last year, on First Full Moon,
The flower market's lanterns were bright as daylight.
The moon rose to the top of the willow tree,
And my love and I met after twilight.

---

[29] For the pronunciation of the character 查 and the possible meaning of the tune-title, see Wen Ju-hsien, pp. 127–28.

[30] *Ibid.*, p. 124. For the authorship of this lyric, see *ibid.*, Introduction, p. 9.

> This year, on First Full Moon,
> Moon and lanterns are the same as last year's.
> But the man of last year—where is he?
> The sleeves of my spring dress are covered with
>   tears.

Note

The original for "First Full Moon" is *yüan-yeh*, abbreviation for *shang-yüan-yeh* ("Upper Prime Night"), which refers to the fifteenth of the First Month of the lunar year. (The fifteenth of the Seventh Month is known as *chung-yüan* or Middle Prime, and the fifteenth of the Tenth Month as *hsia-yüan* or Lower Prime.) The festival of the First Full Moon is also called the Lantern Festival. For further description of this festival see No. 13.

Meter[31]

```
±  +  /  +  -  -  0
干  +  /  -  -  +  a
干  +  /  +  -  -  0
干  +  /  ±  -  +  a

±  +  /  +  -  -  0
±  +  /  -  -  +  a
±  干  /  +  干  -  0
±  +  /  -  -  +  a
```

The above is the pattern observed by most lyricists, but in the present lyric by Ou-yang Hsiu there are several differences from this pattern: line 1 of the first stanza has + - / - + -, and line 1 of the second stanza has - - / - + -. Further, the rhythm of stanza 2, line 2 is + + - / - +, instead of + + / - - +. This illustrates how metrical rhythm can be modified by syntactic rhythm.

Commentary

This poem is a marvel of verbal economy. Its simple structure, based mainly on repetition and contrast, effectively reveals its

[31]Cf. TL, 3, p. 9a; TP, 3, p. 26a; TF, 3, p. 22.

miniature world fraught with human passion and pathos. The contrast between past and present in the human situation is brought home by the sameness of the physical environment then and now, and this sameness is emphasized by the repetition of certain words. Yet the repetition is not effected mechanically but ingeniously. As the seventeenth-century critic Chin Jen-jui (better known as Chin Sheng-t'an) pointed out,[32] the first line of the second stanza repeats the first line of the first stanza with the exception of one word, while the second line of the second stanza recapitulates both line 2 and line 3 of the first stanza. Line 3 of the second stanza repeats once more the words "last year" from the opening line, and line 4 brings on an emotional climax for which all the preceding lines have been a preparation.

We may compare this poem with A. E. Housman's "When first my way to fair I took,"[33] which achieves its poignant effect by a similar structure, although the added irony of the Housman poem (the girl now has money but the young man is no longer there) is not found in the present poem.

No. 7

蝶戀花

獨倚危樓風細細
望極離愁
黯黯生天際
草色山光殘照裡
無人會得憑闌意

---

[32] Chin Jen-jui, p. 216. I am indebted to my colleague Professor John C. Wang for calling my attention to this reference.

[33] Housman, p. 142.

也擬疏狂圖一醉
對酒當歌
強樂還無味
衣帶漸寬都不悔
況伊銷得人憔悴

Tieh Lüan Hua

tu   yi   wei   lou   feng   hsi-hsi   (siei)
alone lean tall building wind   small-small

      wang chi   li-ch'ou
      gaze extreme parting-sorrow

      an-an   sheng t'ien-chi   (tsiäi)
      dark-dark grow   heaven-side

ts'ao se   shan kuang ts'an-chao   li   (lji)
grass color hill light remnant-sunshine inside

wu-jen hui-te   p'ing-lan   yi   (·i)
no-man understand lean-on-rail meaning

yeh ni   shu-k'uang t'u   yi   tsui   (tswi)
also prepare reckless   plan once drunk

      tui   chiu tang ko
      face wine face song

      ch'iang lo   huan wu-wei   (mjwęi)
      forced pleasure   still no-taste

yi-tai chien   k'uan tu pu   hui   (xuâi)
sash   gradually wide   all not regret

k'uang yi   hsiao-te jen   ch'iao-ts'ui (dz'wi)[34]
moreover she worth   man   pine-away

[34]CST, p. 127. T'ang Kuei-chang (III, p. 218) considers this lyric as by
Liu Yung, but in the CST he includes it among Ou-yang's lyrics as well as

Alone, leaning on the high balcony in a soft breeze,
   I gaze as far as I can, as parting sorrow
     Darkly grows from the horizon.
In the fading sun that lights up the grass and the hills,
No one understands why I stand here, leaning on the rails.

I too would like to be reckless and try to get drunk,
   But, facing wine and song,
     I find it dull to force myself to be merry.
My sash is getting looser and looser; still I don't regret:
For her sake, it's worthwhile pining away!

Meter

See No. 2.

Commentary

The strong emotion expressed in this lyric is blended with the natural surroundings, especially in lines 2 and 3, which involve enjambment and some syntactic ambiguity: the phrase *li-ch'ou* ("parting sorrow") in line 2 can be taken both as the object of *wang* ("gaze") and as the subject of *sheng* ("grow") in the next line, thus playing a pivotal role in joining together the speaker's state of mind and what he sees. In other words, parting sorrow is imaginatively visualized as growing from the horizon together with the darkness. The rest of the lyric is more direct in its mode of expression and more colloquial in style. In stanza 2, line 2 is borrowed from a poem by Ts'ao Ts'ao (155–220), but in the earlier poem the line probably means "facing wine, one should sing," whereas here it means "facing wine and facing song," since the word *tang* can mean either "should" or "to face." This is a case of free borrowing from an earlier poet with a slight change of meaning, rather than an allusion, because the original poem is totally different in sentiment and mood from the present one.

---

among Liu's. The style seems more like the former's, and the imagery in lines 2–3 is similar to that in another lyric by Ou-yang in the meter *T'a-so Hsing* (CST, p. 123).

No. 8

蝶戀花

庭院深深深幾許
楊柳堆烟
簾幕無重數
玉勒雕鞍游冶處
樓高不見章台路

雨橫風狂三月暮
門掩黃昏
無計留春住
淚眼問花花不語
亂紅飛過秋千去

Tieh Lüan Hua

| *t'ing-yüan* | *shen-shen* | *shen-chi-hsü* | | *(xiwo)* |
| courtyard | deep-deep | deep-how-much | | |

| | *yang-liu* | *tui* | *yen* | |
| | willow | pile | mist | |

| | *lien-mu* | *wu-ch'ung-shu* | | *(siu)* |
| | curtain | numberless-fold | | |

| *yü* | *le* | *tiao* | *an* | *yu-yeh* | *ch'u* | *(tś'iwo)* |
| jade | bridle | carved | saddle | sensual-pleasure | place | |

| *lou* | *kao* | *pu* | *chien* | *Chang-t'ai* | *lu* | *(luo)* |
| building | high | not | see | Chang-t'ai | road | |

yü	*heng*	*feng*	*k'uang*	*san-yüeh*	*mu*	*(muo)*
rain	rampage	wind	wild	Third-month	evening	

men	*yen*	*huang-hun*
door	close	twilight

wu	*chi*	*liu*	*ch'un*	*chu*	*(d'iu)*
no	plan	keep	spring	stay	

lei	*yen*	*wen*	*hua*	*hua*	*pu*	*yü*	*(ngiwo)*
tear	eye	ask	flower	flower	not	speak	

luan		*hung*	*fei*	*kuo*	*ch'iu-ch'ien*	*ch'ü*	*(k'iwo)*[35]
disorderly		red	fly	pass	swing		go

Deep, deep lies the courtyard—who know how deep?
      The willows pile up mist:
   Endless folds of hanging curtains and screens.
Where bridle of jade and carved saddle are
  seeking pleasure,
From the high chamber, the road to Chang-t'ai
  cannot be seen.

The rain rages and the wind blusters on an April
  evening.
      The door closes twilight in—
   No way to induce Spring to stay.
Tearful eyes ask the flowers; the flowers do
  not speak.
A riot of red whirls away past the garden swing.

Note

St. 1, l. 5. Road to Chang-t'ai. A street near the Chang-t'ai or
Chang Terrace in Ch'ang-an, conventionally used as a euphemism
for the pleasure quarters.

St. 2, l. 1. April. Since there is generally about a month's

---

[35] *Ibid.*, p. 162. This lyric has also been attributed to Feng Yen-ssu, but
its style is closer to Ou-yang's. See Cheng Ch'ien, I, p. 26.

difference between the solar and lunar calendars, I have rendered
the lunar "Third Month" as "April."

Meter

See No. 2.

Commentary

This lyric has been interpreted in various ways. The Ch'ing
critics Chang Hui-yen and Huang Liao-yüan took it as a political
allegory[36] —a view that has been refuted by Wang Kuo-wei.[37]
However, even apart from the allegorical interpretation, opinions
still differ about the meaning of this poem. Chiang Shang-hsien
takes it as an expression of the poet's own emotions,[38] and Hu
Yün-yi thinks that the first stanza describes a young dandy's
search for pleasure, while the second stanza is a courtesan's self-
lament.[39] A third interpretation is offered by Hsia Ch'eng-t'ao:
that the whole lyric is a description of a woman whose husband
has deserted her and is wandering away from home.[40] The last
interpretation seems to me to fit the tone and mood of the lyric
best.

The opening line, by means of its daring triplication of the word
"deep" *(shen)*, evokes a feeling of deep seclusion. This feeling
may be imagined as experienced both by a would-be observer and
by the heroine herself: the former would find the woman remote
and inaccessible, and the latter feels as if the courtyard to which
she is confined were a boundless sea, cut off from the outside
world, the world in which her faithless lover roams. Line 2 is
ambiguous: it could mean that the willows gather mists on them,
or that the willows themselves look like piled-up mists. Perhaps
we can take it both ways at the same time. Further, it is possible
that "willow" is associated with "Chang-t'ai" in line 5 below,
because of the poem "Willow of Chang-t'ai" about a woman

36Chang Hui-yen, p. 9b; T'ang Kuei-chang, IV, pp. 22–23.
37Wang Kuo-wei, I, *hsia*, p. 3b.
38Chiang Shang-hsien, II, pp. 118–19.
39Hu Yün-yi, pp. 31–32.
40Hsia Ch'eng-t'ao and Sheng T'ao-ch'ing, p. 60.

named Liu ("willow").[41] Ambiguity is also present in the relation between line 2 and line 3. We can take line 3 as a metaphorical continuation of line 2 (in other words, the willows look like endless hanging curtains and screens), or take line 3 separately, as a description of actual curtains and screens. The former interpretation seems preferable. Lines 4 and 5 involve further ambiguity, because the absence of pronouns leaves it unclear to whom the lines refer. Chiang Shang-hsien's interpretation of the two lines as an expression of the poet's own wish to visit a singing girl[42] is acceptable only if we agree with him that the whole poem is autobiographical. Hu Yün-yi takes the lines to mean that the heroine, who is a singing girl, cannot see the road down below from her chamber upstairs.[43] This seems unconvincing, for a girl in a room upstairs can hardly be said to be unable to see the road below. Anyway, what would be the point of saying such a thing? It would be better to take line 4 as an imaginary description of the absent husband or lover seeking pleasure far away, and line 5 as the heroine's complaint: "Even though I gaze hard from my high chamber, I cannot see the road leading to the house of pleasure, where he probably is."

In the first line of the second stanza, the raging rain and violent wind may be considered symbolic of the ruthless forces that have ravaged the heroine's life. The next line can mean "the door is closed at twilight," or "the door closes twilight *in*." I prefer the second meaning, for this would suggest that just as twilight is enclosed inside the courtyard, so is the heroine, and neither can escape. Furthermore, she is unable to detain Spring, which refuses to be closed in with her and is going away. In the last two lines, her feelings are unified with the natural environment: the flowers cannot help her, for they themselves are being blown away by the wind past the garden swing—the swing that reminds her of past youthful gaiety, or perhaps (as suggested by Hsia Ch'eng-t'ao)[44] where she and her husband used to frolic together. Like the

[41] See J. J. Y. Liu, I, pp. 111–12.
[42] Chiang Shang-hsien, *loc.cit.*
[43] Hu Yün-yi, *loc.cit.*
[44] Hsia and Sheng, *loc.cit.*

flowers, she too is withering away and she too can only remain silent.

No. 9.

浪淘沙

今日北池遊
漾漾輕舟
波光瀲灩柳條柔
如此春來春又去
白了人頭

好妓好歌喉
不醉難休
勸君滿滿酌金甌
縱使花時常病酒
也是風流

Lang T'ao Sha

chin-jih	*po*	*ch'ih*	*yu*	*(iəu)*
to-day	north	lake	wander	

	yang-yang	*ch'ing*	*chou*	*(tsiəu)*
	stir-ripple	light	boat	

po	*kuang*	*lien-yen*	*liu*	*t'iao*	*jou*	*(n̂ziəu)*
ripple	brightness	join-each-other	willow	twig	soft	

ju-tz'u	*ch'un*	*lai*	*ch'un*	*yu*	*ch'ü*
like-this	spring	come	spring	again	go

	po-liao	*jen*	*t'ou*	*(d'əu)*
	whiten (ed)	man	head	

hao   chi   hao   ko-hou   (ɣəu)
good singing-girl good song-voice

　　pu   tsui   nan   hsiu   (X̌i̯əu)
　　not   drunk   hard   stop

ch'üan chün man-man cho chin ou (·əu)
urge   you   full-full pour gold cup

tsung-shih   hua-shih   ch'ang ping chiu
even-though   flower-time   often   sick wine

　　yeh   shih   feng-liu   (li̯əu)[45]
　　also   is   gaiety

To-day we roam on the northern lake;
　　Rocking, rocking, in a light boat.
The bright ripples spread; the willow twigs hang soft.
As Spring comes and Spring goes again like this,
　　It has turned your hair white.

A fine singing girl with a fine voice—
　　It's hard to stop until you're drunk.
Let me urge you to fill your golden goblet to the brim:
Even if you are often sick with wine in the season of
　　flowers,
　　　　That's a kind of gaiety too!

Meter[46]

```
      干  +  /  +  -  -  A
         干  +  -  -  A
   干  -  ±  +  /  +  -  -  A
 ±  +  ±  -  /  -  +  +  0
         ±  +  -  -  A

         ±  +  /  +  -  -  A
         干  +  -  -  A
 ±  -  干  +  /  +  -  -  A
 干  +  ±  -  /  -  +  +  0
         干  +  -  -  A
```

[45] CST, p. 141.
[46] Cf. TL, 1, p. 13b; TP, 10, p. 20b; TF, 5 *hsia*, p. 46b.

Commentary

This is a light-hearted song on the familiar theme of *carpe diem*. The gaiety of the poet's mood is conveyed through the straight-forward language and the lilting rhythm, emphasized by the use of reduplications (*yang-yang* in stanza 1, line 2; *man-man* in stanza 2, line 3), repetitions (of the word *ch'un* in stanza 1, line 3; of the word *hao* in stanza 2, line 1), and a rhyming disyllable (*lien-yen* or *liäm-iäm* in stanza 1, line 2).

When we turn to a general discussion of Ou-yang Hsiu as a lyricist, our task is complicated by problems of authorship with regard to a number of lyrics. Among the more than two hundred lyrics attributed to him, there are several dozen that also appear in the collected lyrics of other poets such as Yen Shu and Liu Yung. Some of these have been demonstrated to be not Ou-yang's works, and others may be accepted as his. In either case, these lyrics are so similar to the majority of Ou-yang's lyrics that the question of their authorship does not greatly affect our impression and evaluation of his lyrics as a corpus. A more serious problem is the authorship of seventy-three lyrics that are not included in the earliest known edition of his lyrics (part of his *Complete Works* first published in 1196), but appear in a later edition of unknown origin.[47] Since many of these are strongly erotic in nature and highly colloquial in style, traditional critics have generally considered them spurious and even asserted that they were forged by the poet's enemies to besmear his name.[48] On the other hand, some modern scholars, notably Tanaka Kenji, have expressed their belief in the authenticity of these lyrics.[49]

---

[47]The *Complete Works* refers to the *Ou-yang Wen-chung kung ch'üan-chi* 歐陽文忠公全集, of which *chüan* 131–133 consist of *tz'u* and are labelled *chin-t'i yüeh-fu* 近體樂府. The later edition is the *Tsui-weng ch'in-ch'ü wai-pien* 醉翁琴趣外編. See Jao Tsung-yi, I, pp. 37-40.

[48]See Wu Shih-tao, p. 2a; Shen Hsiung, *shang*, p. 15; Wang Yi-ch'ing, I, 114, pp. 6b–7a.

[49]Tanaka, pp. 50–62; Lu and Feng, pp. 622–24; Liu Ta-chieh, *chung*, p. 228. Others who accept Ou-yang's authorship of these lyrics include Feng Ch'i-yung (p. 143) and T'ang Kuei-chang (CST). Cheng Ch'ien (I, p. 25) says that one must consider them separately, but does not explain how to tell the authentic ones from the fakes.

It seems to me that although there is no inherent impossibility of Ou-yang's authorship of these lyrics, their genuineness has not been proved beyond doubt. As long as this remains true, any general observations on his lyrics must be understood to be not necessarily applicable to those of questioned authorship. And even if these should be proved to be his, they would still form only a small proportion of his lyrics and could not be taken as typical of his lyric poetry as a whole.

Ou-yang's lyrics are on the whole similar to Yen Shu's, but there are some differences. First, the former have a wider scope and explore more varied and less confined worlds than do the latter. In Ou-yang's lyrics, we see something of the grandeur of Nature, not just its intimate aspects, although its more awe-inspiring aspects are still absent. For example, in No. 9 above, and in a series of thirteen lyrics he wrote to the tune *Ts'ai Sang Tzu*[50] to describe the scenery of the West Lake at Ying-chou, there is a feeling of wide-open space and carefree enjoyment, a feeling we seldom get from Yen's lyrics. Secondly, Ou-yang shows a more wholehearted attitude towards life, a greater readiness to surrender himself to the mood of the moment. Consequently his lyrics are emotionally more powerful and less restrained than Yen's. Furthermore, Ou-yang has a deeper insight into feminine psychology. Some of his lyrics (such as Nos. 5, 6, and 8 above) describe the imagined emotions of women with considerable sympathetic understanding, so that we feel we are enabled to share their feelings, not merely invited to look at them with admiration. Inevitably, some commentators have found it necessary to insist that these lyrics are political allegories!

Ou-yang's diction is similar to Yen's: elegant and natural, sometimes colloquial but rarely slangy (if we disregard those lyrics of questionable authorship). Allusions are few, and these few are all familiar, not obscure. However, Ou-yang does borrow quite freely from earlier poets. The borrowing from Ts'ao Ts'ao in No. 7 we have already noted. There are also several lyrics that contain lines derived from Li Shang-yin (813–858). For instance, the phrase "wanton leaves and seductive twigs" in one lyric[51] is

[50]CST, pp. 121–22.
[51]*Ibid.*, p. 135.

taken from one of Li's "Terrace of Yen" poems,[52] and the following lines from another lyric

> The cold waves do not move; the bamboo mat is flat.
> A pair of crystal pillows—
> Besides which lies a fallen hairpin[53]

are derived from Li's "Casual Lines":

> By the amber pillow on the water-patterned bamboo mat
> Lies a fallen hairpin with a pair of kingfishers'
> feathers.[54]

It is interesting that although Ou-yang Hsiu is considered one of the first Sung poets to have reacted against the Hsi-k'un School of poets who imitated Li Shang-yin, and to have evolved a new style of poetry in the *shih* form,[55] he was not averse to borrow from Li when writing lyrics. This shows how Ou-yang regarded the lyric as a medium that was suited to such themes as love, themes for which an ornate diction was appropriate (since many of Li's poems deal with love and use an ornate diction), but reserved the *shih* for more public themes that he thought required a more austere language.

Syntactically, Ou-yang Hsiu's lyrics do not present many striking features. Enjambment occurs only occasionally, such as in lines 2 and 3 in No. 7 above, and in the following lines from two other lyrics:

所 恨 征 輪
漸 漸 成 迢 遞

| *so* | *hen* | *cheng* | *lun* |
| that-which | resent | travel | wheel |

| *chien-chien* | *ch'eng* | *t'iao-ti*[56] |
| gradually | journey | long-stretching |

[52] Feng Hao, 5, p. 34a; J. J. Y. Liu, II, p. 67.
[53] CST, p. 140.
[54] Feng Hao, 5, p. 15b; J. J. Y. Liu, II, p. 81.
[55] Yoshikawa, I, pp. 60–62, 72.
[56] CST, p. 128.

What I resent is the travelling carriage
Which gradually went farther and farther away.

況 有 笙 歌
艷 態 相 縈 繞

k'uang	yu	sheng	ko
moreover	there-are	pipe	song

yen	t'ai	hsiang	jung-jao[57]
beautiful	appearance	(prefix)	surround

Moreover, there are pipes and songs
And beautiful girls surrounding me.

Metrically, Ou-yang's lyrics do not show great variety. If we exclude those lyrics of disputed authorship, we find altogether thirty-nine meters, of which thirty-three are "little airs" and only six are "slow lyrics." The longest of them consists of one hundred and sixteen syllables, the shortest of thirty-six.[58] If, on the other hand, we include the lyrics the authorship of which has been questioned, then the total number of meters used is seventy-three, of which fifty-five are "little airs" and eighteen are "slow lyrics." These comparative statistics suggest that if he really wrote those lyrics in question, then he was much more of an experimentor in metrical forms than he would otherwise appear to be.

Ou-yang's use of imagery resembles Yen Shu's. Among images of comparison, those likening one physical object to another tend to be commonplace, such as the comparison of the windless surface of water to smooth glass.[59] Images that compare human emotions to physical objects are more effective, such as:

The farther you go, the more endless grows
    parting sorrow:
Stretching on and on, unbroken like the spring water.[60]

[57] *Ibid.*
[58] The longest is *Mo-yü-erh*, the shortest *Ch'ang Hsiang-ssu*.
[59] CST, pp. 121, 143.
[60] *Ibid.*, p. 123.

What is this feeling like?
Fine like light silk threads, stretching far like waves.[61]

Some images involve implicit or explicit puns. In the line

Her heart is like weaving[62]

the image arouses associations with weaving silk (*ssu* 絲), which puns on the word *ssu* (思 , "thought" or "longing"). The same pun becomes explicit in the following lines, where "silk thread" (*ssu*) refers to the filament in the stem of the lotus. At the same time, the word for lotus, *lien* 蓮 , is a pun on the word *lien* 憐 , which means "love."

The lotus stem (love) is broken, the silk thread
(thought) drags on;
For this alone she falls into a wistful mood.[63]

A similar example occurs in the next lines (put in the mouth of a young girl):

The lotus seed and myself are always alike:
No nice feelings—
Year after year, only bitterness in the heart.[64]

Here the comparison of the girl's heart to the lotus seed rests on the puns on *lien* ("lotus" and "love"), *k'u* ("bitterness" both in the literal and the metaphorical senses), and *hsin* (meaning both "heart" and "center").

In short, Ou-yang did not greatly extend the scope of the lyric, but within the limits of the genre as he understood it, he achieved high standards of excellence.

[61] *Ibid.*, p. 124.
[62] *Ibid.*, p. 130.
[63] *Ibid.*, p. 127.
[64] *Ibid.*, p. 130.

CHAPTER 2

Emotional Realism and Stylistic Innovations

Liu Yung (fl. 1034)[1] and Ch'in Kuan (1049-1100)

Although Liu Yung was a contemporary of Yen Shu and Ou-yang Hsiu, his works opened a new era in the history of the lyric while theirs mainly followed an earlier tradition. It is therefore appropriate to deal with his poetry after theirs. Liu's epoch-making significance lies in his introduction of a new realism in the expression of emotion, a much freer use of colloquial language than previously seen, and various stylistic and prosodic innovations. Among those influenced by him, Ch'in Kuan is generally considered a major lyricist in his own right, and may be discussed in the same chapter.

The circumstances of these two poets' lives were not dissimilar—both had unsuccessful official careers and knew the bitterness of exile, but each reacted to these circumstances very differently.[2] Whereas Ch'in Kuan was involved in the struggle between political factions and remained a Confucian in public life, Liu Yung flouted Confucian moral standards and seems to have been unconcerned with politics. Indeed, he spent much of his life in the company of courtesans, and many of his lyrics were written for them to sing, probably dashed off at gay parties. This may account for the carelessness and repetitiousness of some of his lyrics. However, other lyrics by him show great mastery of poetic skill and are obviously the results of concentrated efforts.

---

[1] The dates of Liu Yung's birth and death are not known for certain. T'ang Kuei-chang (II, pp. 91–98; III, p. 17) gives 987 and 1053, based on circumstantial evidence. Chiang Shang-hsien (II, p. 137) gives 1004?–1063?, without quoting any authority. The only definite date about Liu's life is the year he passed the *chin-shih* examination, 1034.

[2] For Liu's life, see T'ang Kuei-chang, II. For Ch'in's, see SS, *chüan* 444.

No. 10   Liu Yung

柳　永
雨　霖　鈴

寒蟬淒切
對長亭晚
驟雨初歇
都門帳飲無緒
方留戀處
蘭舟催發
執手相看淚眼
竟無語凝咽
念去去千里烟波
暮靄沈沈楚天闊

多情自古傷離別
更那堪冷落清秋節
今宵酒醒何處
楊柳岸曉風殘月
此去經年
應是良辰
美景虛設
便縱有千種風情
更與何人說

Yü Lin Ling

han   ch'an   ch'i-ch'ieh   (ts'iet)
cold   cicada   chilly-sad

tui   ch'ang-t'ing   wan
face   long-pavilion   evening

chou-yü   ch'u   hsieh   (χiͮt)
sudden-rain   just   stop

tu   men   chang-yin   wu-hsü
capital   gate   tent-drink   listless

fang   liu-lüan   ch'u
just   linger   place

lan   chou   ts'ui   fa   (pi̮wͮt)
magnolia   boat   urge   set-out

chih   shou   hsiang   k'an   lei   yen
hold   hand   mutual   look   tear   eye

ching   wu-yü   ning   yeh   ('iet)
even   no-speech   freeze   sob

nien   ch'ü-ch'ü   ch'ien-li   yen   po
think   depart-depart   thousand-mile   mist   wave

mu   ai   ch'en-ch'en   Ch'u   t'ien   k'uo   (k'uât)
evening   cloud   deep-deep   Ch'u   sky   wide

to-ch'ing   tzu-ku   shang   li-pieh   (piät)
loving-ones   since-antiquity   lament   parting

keng   na-k'an   leng-lo   ch'ing   ch'iu   chieh   (tsiet)
moreover   how-bear   desolate   cool   autumn   season

chin-hsiao   chiu   hsing   ho-ch'u
to-night   wine   wake   what-place

yang-liu   an   hsiao   feng   ts'an   yüeh   (ngiwͮt)
willow   bank   dawn   wind   remnant   moon

tz'u-ch'ü   ching-nien
this-departure   year-after-year

details help create a forlorn atmosphere, while the mention of the post-pavilion immediately arouses associations with parting, since it was customary to see friends and relatives off at such pavilions. This is followed up by line 4, which reveals the poet's listless feelings at the farewell party. Lines 5–10 directly depict the parting scene. The poet first describes his own reluctance to depart, then the unbearable grief felt both by himself and by his beloved, and finally his anticipation of the long, lonely journey ahead.

In the second stanza, the poet universalizes his emotions by referring to the countless lovers who have suffered parting sorrows since antiquity, thus justifying his own state of mind and engaging our sympathy for him. He further anticipates the future, developing the train of thought started in lines 9–10 of the previous stanza. Line 4 conjures up a whole world of loneliness, nostalgia, and depression by means of a few clearly visualized and sharply drawn simple images. The fusion of emotion and scene is perfectly achieved.

In this lyric Liu Yung successfully blends conventional poetic diction with colloquialisms. The expressions *ch'ang-t'ing* ("long pavilion"), *chang-yin* ("tent-drink"), *lan chou* ("magnolia boat"), *Ch'u t'ien* ("Ch'u sky," i.e., Southern sky), and *liang-ch'en mei-ching* ("fine hours and beautiful views") are all derived from earlier literature, but since they are common expressions, they cannot be considered allusions. They are rather part and parcel of conventional poetic language, here woven unobtrusively into the poetic texture. On the other hand, the colloquial words, like *yen* for "eyes," *na* for "how," *shih* for "be," *pien* for "even," and *shuo* for "speak," add a conversational touch to the diction. The combined effects of the two kinds of diction are felt in the general tone, which is straightforward and informal, without being stilted on the one hand or undignified on the other.

As befits such a tone, the imagery is also simple and unobtrusive. The only possible compound image is "frozen sobs" *(ning-yeh)*, although even here some readers may not wish to take the word *ning* ("frozen") literally. I have chosen to take *ning* literally as "frozen" and the whole phrase as a compound image of comparison, because this is Liu Yung's original invention and not a conventional, fossilized image. The other images in this poem are all simple, achieving their effect through their sensuous appeal and emotional associations rather than by unexpected comparisons or startling juxtapositions. The versification also contributes to the informal style of the poem. Enjambment occurs so often that at times it is difficult to say where one "line" ends and another begins. Syntactically, in the first stanza, lines 1–3, 5–6, 7–8, and 9–10 may be considered complete sentences, and in the second stanza, lines 1–2, 5–7 (5–6 if we take lines 6 and 7 as one line, as some scholars do), and 8–9 (or 7–8). The end of each sentence generally coincides with a rhyme. Thus the whole poem has an unbroken rhythmic flow, punctuated by somewhat widely scattered rhymes. This rhythm has an effect very different from that produced by clear-cut, end-stopped lines with a quick succession of rhymes: instead of calling our attention to a few details, it leads us on like a meandering stream. Not only is there a fluent rhythm throughout the poem, but there is also considerable rhythmic flexibility within the line. For example, lines 1, 2, and 5 in the first stanza are all tetra-syllabic, but each has a different rhythm according to the meaning and syntax. Line 1 has a 2:2 rhythm (--/++), line 2 a 1:2:1 rhythm (+/--/+), and line 5, a 1:3 rhythm (-/-++). The suppleness of the verse is also enhanced by the use of the initial mono-syllabic segment. Lines 2, 5, 8, and 9 in stanza 1 and lines 2 and 7 in stanza 2 all begin with monosyllabic words. With one exception (line 5, stanza 1), these monosyllables all have Oblique Tones and light stresses. Each of them introduces a subtle variation in rhythm by creating a slight pause, and sometimes acts as a link with the preceding line, thereby further blurring the division between lines and increasing the smooth flow of the rhythm. The auditory effect of the lyric is still further enriched by alliterative and rhyming disyllables (*ch'i-ch'ieh* or *ts'iei-ts'iet* in stanza 1, line 1; *liu-lüan* or *liəu-liwän* in line 5; *leng-lo* or *lɒng-lak* in stanza 2, line 2; *han-ch'an* or *ɣan-ẓïän* in stanza 1, line 1) and reduplica-tions (*ch'ü-ch'ü* or *k'iu-k'iu* in stanza 1, line 9; *ch'en-ch'en* or *â'iəm-â'iəm* in line 10). The rhythmic pattern of the whole poem is well suited to the explicit and expansive mode of expression, which in turn reflects the poet's frank and direct attitude towards experience.

No. 11

八聲甘州

對瀟瀟暮雨灑江天
一番洗清秋
漸霜風凄緊
關河冷落
殘照當樓
是處紅衰翠減
苒苒物華休
惟有長江水
無語東流

不忍登高臨遠
望故鄉渺邈
歸思難收
嘆年來蹤跡
何事苦淹留
想佳人
妝樓顒望
誤幾回
天際識歸舟
爭知我
倚闌干處
正恁凝愁

Pa-sheng Kan-chou

tui	hsiao-hsiao	mu	yü	sa	chiang	t'ien
facing	(sound of rain)	evening	rain	sprinkle	river	sky

yi-fan   hsi   ch'ing   ch'iu   (ts'i̯ə̯u)
once   wash   cool   autumn

chien   shuang   feng   ch'i   chin
gradually   frost   wind   chilly   hard

kuan-ho   leng-lo
mountain-pass-river   desolate

ts'an-chao   tang   lou   (lə̯u)
remnant-sunshine   face   building

shih-ch'u   hung   shuai   ts'ui   chien
everywhere   red   fade   green   decrease

jan-jan   wu-hua   hsiu   (χi̯ə̯u)
gradually   thing-splendor   cease

wei-yu   Ch'ang-chiang   shui
only   Long-River   water

wu-yü   tung   liu   (li̯ə̯u)
no-word   east   flow

pu   jen   teng   kao   lin   yüan
not   bear   climb   high   overlook   far

wang   ku-hsiang   miao   miao
gaze   old-country   dim   distant

kuei-ssu   nan   shou   (śi̯ə̯u)
return-thought   hard   stop

t'an   nien-lai   tsung-chi
sigh   since-last-year   foot-print

ho-shih   k'u   yen-liu   (li̯ə̯u)
what-for   painfully   linger

 hsiang   chia-jen
 imagine   beautiful-person

chuang-lou   yung   wang
dressing-chamber   raise-head gaze

   wu   chi-hui
   mistake how-many-times

t'ien-chi shih   kuei   chou   (tśịạu)
sky-side   recognize   return boat

   cheng chih   wo
   how   know   I

yi   lan-kan   ch'u
lean railing   place

cheng jen   ning   ch'ou   (dz'ịạu)[5]
just   thus freeze sorrow

Facing me, the blustering evening rain besprinkles the
sky over the river,
    Washing the cool autumn air once more.
Gradually, the frosty wind rises chilly and hard,
    The landscape looks more forlorn,
    The fading sun falls on the balcony.
Everywhere, the red withers and the green fades away:
    One by one, the glories of Nature cease.
    Only the water of the Long River
    Flows in silence to the east.

I cannot bear to climb high and look far,
    For to gaze at my native land in the dim distance
    Would release endless homeward thoughts.
I sigh over the past year's wanderings;
Why should I desperately linger on?
    I imagine the fair one
    Is now gazing, head raised, from her chamber.
    How often has she

[5]CST, p. 43.

Mistaken a returning boat on the horizon for mine?
How would she know that I,
Leaning here on the railings,
Should be congealed with sorrow like this?

Note

St. 1, l. 8. Long River. The Yangtze.

Meter[6]

```
+  Ŧ  -  /  ±  +  +  -  -  0
   ±  Ŧ  /  +  -  -  A
   +  /  Ŧ  -  -  +  0
      -  -  ±  +  0
      Ŧ  +  -  -  A
±  +  /  Ŧ  -  ±  +  0
   ±  +  /  +  -  -  A
   Ŧ  +  /  -  -  +  0
      Ŧ  +  -  -  A

      ±  +  /  Ŧ  -  Ŧ  +  0
      ±  /  +  -  ±  +  0
         Ŧ  +  -  -  A
      +  /  Ŧ  -  Ŧ  +  0
      Ŧ  +  /  +  -  -  A
            +  -  -  0
         Ŧ  -  Ŧ  +  0
            +  ±  -  0
      Ŧ  +  +  -  -  A
            -  -  +  0
      ±  -  Ŧ  +  0
      ±  +  -  -  A
```

Commentary

The first stanza is mainly concerned with depicting the external scene, and the second stanza concentrates on the emotions of the

[6]Cf. TL, 1, p. 18a; TP, 25, p. 5b; TF, 1, p. 34a.

poet.   Yet these two aspects of the poetic world are closely integrated, for in the first stanza the scene described already suggests the emotions to be expressed in the next stanza, whereas the second stanza paints an imaginary scene created by the emotions. More specifically, in stanza 1 the gloomy atmosphere produced by the bleak landscape is emphasized by such words as *ch'i* ("chilly and sad"), *ts'an* ("remnant, fading"), *shuai* ("wither"), and *chien* ("decrease, fade").   In the second stanza, the poet juxtaposes the actual scene (himself leaning on the railing of the balcony and gazing at the horizon) with the imaginary scene (his beloved gazing at the horizon from her chamber), thereby revealing the quiet but deep feelings of homesickness and yearning for his beloved. Furthermore, the poem is not confined to one time or one place, although it may seem to describe only the present view and mood. In the first stanza, the first two lines, as indicated by the word *tui* ("facing") at the beginning, have to be taken as describing the present scene, yet the word *chien* ("gradually"), which is introduced at the beginning of line 3 but governs not only line 3 but also lines 4 and 5, makes it necessary for us to assume that there is a lapse of time, for otherwise the mention of sunshine in line 5 would contradict the description of rain in line 1.   In this manner we are made aware of the gradual passing of time and the changes taking place in the landscape.   In the second stanza, by imagining his beloved to be gazing at the horizon and longing for him just as he is gazing at the horizon and longing for her, the poet obliterates the barriers of space and brings together "here" and "there." Moreover, since she is said to have mistaken someone else's homeward-bound boat as his many times before, she is pictured not only as gazing at the horizon at this very moment but also as having done so countless times before.   Thus, "past" and "present" are also brought together.

The diction of this lyric is again simple and straightforward, combining conventional poetic language with colloquial expressions.   Among conventional phrases are *kuan-ho* ("mountain-passes and rivers"), a variation of *shan-ho* ("mountains and rivers"), which is a common way of referring to landscape; *wu-hua* ("thing-splendor"), meaning the beauties of Nature; and *chia-jen* ("beautiful person"). Colloquial words include *yi-fan* ("once"), *chi-hui* ("how many times"), *cheng* ("how"), and *jen* ("thus"). No allusions are used, although, as commentators have pointed out, there are echoes of earlier poets. Stanza 1, line 6, is derived from Li Shang-yin's poem "To the Lotus",[7] and stanza 2, line 7, is derived from Hsieh T'iao (464-94),[8] with a possible echo of Wen T'ing-yün (812-70?) as well.[9] These derived expressions do not stand out as unassimilated elements but blend well with their contexts.

The imagery is simple but effective because of its strong visual appeal. Despite the absence of compound images or elaborate, colorful details, the succession of simple images paints a scene and evokes a mood as effectively as a landscape painting in ink by a Sung or Yüan master.

In versification, there are several notable features. First, we may note the use of onomatopoeia (*hsiao-hsiao* or *sieu-sieu* in stanza 1, line 1, imitating the sound of wind and rain), reduplication (*jan-jan* or *ńźiäm-ńźiäm* in stanza 1, line 7), and alliteration (*miao-miao* or *miau-mâk* in stanza 2, line 2). Next, we may note the effect of enjambment, which occurs throughout the poem (stanza 1, lines 1-2, 3-5, 8-9; stanza 2, lines 1-3, 4-5, 6-9, 10-12), and produces a flowing rhythm unbroken by clear-cut line-divisions. Finally, the use of the initial monosyllabic segment is striking and involves some unusual syntactic structures. Sometimes the initial monosyllable functions as a verb (as in stanza 1, line 1, and stanza 2, lines 2, 4, and 6), and sometimes as an adverb (as in stanza 1, line 3). When used as a verb, the monosyllabic segment may have the rest of the line as its object (as in stanza 2, line 2), or even include the next line as part of its object (as in stanza 1, lines 1-2, and stanza 2, lines 4-5, 6-7). When used as an adverb, the monosyllabic segment is placed before the subject instead of after it (which is the normal word-order), and governs several lines (stanza 1, lines 3-5). Such uses of the initial monosyllable increase the syntactic flexibility and rhythmic variety of the poem.

[7]See Hu Yün-yi, p. 44.
[8]*Ibid.* Also, Hsia and Sheng, p. 64; Chiang Shang-hsien, II, p. 146.
[9]Hu Yün-yi, p. 44; Cheng Ch'ien, I, p. 37.

No. 12

夜半樂

凍雲黯淡天氣
扁舟一葉
乘興離江渚
渡萬壑千岩
越溪深處
怒濤漸息
樵風乍起
更聞商旅相呼
片帆高舉
泛畫鷁
翩翩過南浦

望中酒斾閃閃
一簇烟村
數行霜樹
殘日下
漁人鳴榔歸去
敗荷零落
衰楊掩映
岸邊兩兩三三
浣紗遊女
避行客
含羞笑相語

到此因念
繡閣輕抛
浪萍難駐
嘆後約
丁寧竟何據
慘離懷
空恨歲晚歸期阻
凝淚眼
杳杳神京路
斷鴻聲遠長天暮

Yeh-pan Yüeh

tung   *yün*   *an-tan*   *t'ien-ch'i*
frozen   cloud   dark-gloomy   sky-air

   p'ien   *chou*   *yi*   *yeh*
   tiny   boat   one   leaf

ch'eng   *hsing*   *li*   *chiang*   *chu*   *(tśiwo)*
take-advantage-of   high-spirit   leave   river   islet

tu   *wan*   *ho*   *ch'ien*   *yen*
pass   myriad   valley   thousand   cliff

   Yüeh   *hsi*   *shen*   *ch'u*   *(tśiwo)*
   Yüeh   stream   deep   place

   nu   *t'ao*   *chien*   *hsi*
   angry   wave   gradually   stop

ch'iao-feng   *cha*   *ch'i*
firewood-wind   suddenly   rise

keng   wen   shang-lü   hsiang   hu
again   hear   merchant-traveller   mutually   call

   p'ien-fan   kao   chü   (kịwo)
   one-piece-sail   high   raise

      fan   hua-yi
      drift   painted-fishhawk

  p'ien-p'ien   kuo   nan   p'u   (p'uo)
  flutter   pass   south   shore

wang-chung   chiu-p'ei   shan-shan
gaze-inside   wine-banner   gleam

   yi-ts'u   yen   ts'un
   one-cluster   mist   village

   shu   hang   shuang   shu   (źịu)
   several   row   frost   tree

      ts'an   jih   hsia
      remnant   sun   under

yü-jen   ming   lang   kuei-ch'ü   (k'ịwo)
fisherman   sound   pole   go-back

   pai   ho   ling-lo
   faded   lotus   fall-away

   shuai   yang   yen-ying
   withered   willow   covered-shining

an-pien   liang-liang   san-san
bank-side   two-two   three-three

   huan   sha   yu-nü   (nịwo)
   wash   silk-gauze   wander-girl

      pi   hsing   k'e
      avoid   travel   stranger

  han-hsiu   hsiao   hsiang   yü   (ngịwo)
  with-shyness   laugh   mutually   talk

tao   *tz'u*   *yin*   *nien*
arrive here therefore think

hsiu   *ke*   *ch'ing*   *p'ao*
embroidered room lightly desert

lang   *p'ing*   *nan*   *chu*   *(t̯iu)*
roaming duckweed hard stay

t'an   *hou-yüeh*
sigh later-appointment

ting-ning   *ching*   *ho*   *chü*   *(k̯iwo)*
repeatedly-tell finally what basis

ts'an   *li-huai*
sad separation-bosom

k'ung   *hen*   *sui*   *wan*   *kuei-ch'i*   *tsu*   *(ts̯iwo)*
in-vain resent year late return-date delay

ning   *lei*   *yen*
fix tear eye

miao-miao   *shen-ching*   *lu*   *(luo)*
far-far divine-capital road

tuan   *hung*   *sheng*   *yüan*   *ch'ang*   *t'ien*   *mu*   *(muo)*[10]
cut-off wild-goose sound far long sky evening

Frozen clouds in the dark gloomy air—
    In a tiny leaf of a boat
  I left the river islet in high spirits.
  Passing a myriad valleys and a thousand cliffs,
    I sailed where the Yüeh stream ran deep.
    The angry waves gradually calmed,
    The forest wind suddenly rose.
Then I heard the travelling merchants calling to
  one another.
    Hoisting high my single sail,
      I drifted on in the "painted fishhawk"
  Which fluttered past the southern shore.

[10]CST, p. 37.

Now a gleaming tavern's sign comes into view,
    Then a cluster of misty villages,
    And several rows of frosty trees.
      In the fading sun,
Fishermen, knocking their boats with poles,
    return home.
      Faded lotus leaves fall away,
      Withering willows shimmer faintly.
On the bank, in twos and threes,
      The girls washing their silk clothes
        Avoid the travelling stranger
    While shyly laughing and talking among themselves.

      Coming here makes me think:
      "I've too easily deserted her chamber;
      Now the drifting duckweed can hardly stop!"
        I sigh over the date of our reunion,
    Which she kept telling me to remember—Can
    it be counted on after all?
        My heart saddened by separation—
Useless to resent that it is late in the year and
    my return has been delayed.
      I fix my tearful eyes
      On the road that stretches far, far towards
      the capital.
A stray wild goose cries in the distance; the vast
    sky darkens.

Notes

St. 1, l. 5. Yüeh stream. Identified by commentators with the
Jo-yeh stream situated in the ancient kingdom of Yüeh (modern
Chekiang). The famous beauty Hsi Shih (fifth century B.C.) is
said to have washed silk gauze in this stream when she was a
village girl. Later she was presented by the King of Yüeh to his
old enemy the King of Wu, and wrought the latter's downfall.

l. 7. Forest wind. The original is *ch'iao feng,* literally "firewood
wind."   Hu Yün-yi explains this as "mountain wind,"[11] and

[11] Hu Yün-yi, p. 43.

Chiang Shang-hsien as "autumn wind."[12]   Neither quotes any supporting evidence. I fail to see why the phrase cannot simply mean "forest wind."

l. 10. Painted fishhawk. Boats were painted with the fishhawk on the prow as an auspicious sign, since this bird is strong in flight and not afraid of the wind. Consequently, "painted fishhawk" became a common literary substitute for a boat.

l. 11. Southern shore. A conventional poetic phrase associated with farewell.

St. 2, l. 5. Knocking their boats. It is said that fishermen knocked their boats with long poles to startle the fish so that they would leap into the net.

l. 9. The line literally says, "Wandering girls washing silk gauze." The word "wandering" cannot be taken literally, since these are obviously local girls and not wanderers. However, the word often has the connotation of "wandering for pleasure," and it seems reasonable to suppose that the poet uses it here to suggest that the girls are lighthearted, like people on a pleasure trip. As for "washing silk gauze," this alludes to Hsi Shih (mentioned above), and should not be taken too literally but rather as a conventionally poetic way of saying "washing their clothes."

St. 3, l. 2. Chamber. The original has *hsiu ke,* literally "embroidered chamber." Because this is a purely conventional expression meaning simply a lady's chamber, I have omitted the adjective in the translation.

l. 9. Capital. The original has "divine capital" *(shen ching).* Again I have omitted the conventional adjective, which would create a misleading impression if translated literally.

Meter[13]

```
+  -  /  +  +  -  +  0
      -  -  +  +  0
   -  +  /  -  -  +  a
+  /  +  +  -  -  0
   +  -  -  +  a
   +  -  +  +  0
```

[12]Chiang Shang-hsien, II, p. 142.
[13]Cf. TL, 20, p. 15b; TP, 38, p. 13a; TF, 4 *hsia,* pp. 40a–b.

```
          -   -   +   +   a'
  +   -   /   -   +   -   -   0
          +   -   -   +   a
              +   +   +   0
      -   -   /   +   -   +   a
  +   -   /   +   +   +   +   0
              +   +   -   -   0
              +   -   -   +   a
                  -   +   +   0
  -   -   /   -   -   -   +   a
          +   -   -   +   0
          -   -   +   +   0
  +   -   /   +   +   -   -   0
          +   -   -   +   a
          +   -   +   0
      -   -   /   +   -   +   a

          +   +   -   +   0
          +   +   -   -   0
          +   -   -   +   a
          +   +   +   0
      -   -   /   +   -   +   a
  -   +   +   +   /   -   -   +   a
          -   +   +   0
      +   +   -   -   +   a
  +   -   -   +   /   -   -   +   a
```

There are only two known lyrics written to the tune *Yeh-pan Yüeh*. Both are by Liu Yung, but each has a somewhat different metrical pattern. Thus, the present lyric may be considered a unique specimen.

The use of the final *i* to rhyme with *iwo, iu* and *uo* suggests that Liu Yung rhymed rather freely.[14] I have marked *i* with *a'* to show that it does not belong to the same rhyme category as *iwo, uo,* and *iu.*

[14] See Wang Li, pp. 555–56.

Commentary

The world of this poem is a dynamic one: first we accompany the poet, retrospectively, on his journey (in stanza 1); then we follow the movements of his roaming gaze (in stanza 2) and the directions of his wandering thoughts (in stanza 3). The mode of presentation, especially in the first two stanzas, is comparable to that of the cinema. The first stanza is a flashback. We see the poet embarking on his journey, and we view the landscape as if from a fleeting boat, not statically. Apart from the opening line, which foreshadows the melancholy atmosphere of the next two stanzas, the first stanza gives us a feeling of exhilaration, emphasized by various verbs denoting action and movement, such as *li* ("leave"), *tu* ("pass"), *ch'i* ("rise"), *chü* ("hoist"), *fan* ("drift"), and *p'ien-p'ien* ("flutter").

The second stanza begins with a closeup of the banner used as a tavern's sign, gleaming in the setting sun and tempting the weary traveller to stop for a drink. Then the camera shifts its focus to objects in the more distant background, and the scenery becomes increasingly depressing: the "frosty" trees, the "fading" sun, the "faded" lotus leaves, and the "withering" willows. The only cheerful sight is that of the girls, yet, ironically, since they shy away from the stranger and exclude him from their world of laughter and talk, he is made to feel more conscious of his solitude and to think of the woman he has left behind. Thus, the transition from seemingly objective description of scenery to overtly subjective expression of emotion is immediately yet naturally made, and the poem moves on smoothly to the last stanza.

In the third stanza, as Chiang Shang-hsien has observed,[15] the lady's chamber is suggested by the girls mentioned in the previous stanza, and the drifting duckweed by the faded lotus leaves. Having thus introduced his neglected love and his own aimless wandering, the poet then goes on unashamedly to express his homesickness and loneliness. The stray wild goose crying far away in the last line does not, I think, represent the absence of letters, as Hu Yün-yi says[16] (though it is common enough in

[15] Chiang Shang-hsien, II, p. 142.
[16] Hu Yün-yi, p. 43.

Chinese poetry to use the wild goose to represent a messenger). Rather, it is another symbol of isolation, bewilderment, and exile. The final words echo the opening line and bring the whole poem to a close on a note of gloom.

The language of the poem is simple but relatively "literary," with few colloquialisms but quite a number of conventional phrases, images, and allusions. Some of these conventional expressions, such as "embroidered chamber" and "southern shore," add little to the poetic effect. But others, because of their associations or their contexts, are quite effective. For instance, the comparison of a tiny boat to a single leaf is a conventional image, and when we first read "in a tiny leaf of a boat" *(p'ien-chou yi-yeh)*, it does not strike us with particular force; but when we come to the "drifting duckweed" *(lang p'ing)*, we sense an underlying unity between the two, since both belong to the same order of things in Nature, and both represent the poet's wanderings. Furthermore, there is also some underlying coherence between the "drifting duckweed" and the "faded lotus leaves," as suggested above. In this way, the metaphorical reality represented by the leaf and the duckweed becomes submerged in the actual reality represented by the lotus leaves, and each enriches the other. Similarly, the "painted fishhawk" *(hua-yi)* is a common substitute for a boat, but when it is followed by "flutter" *(p'ien-p'ien)*, it becomes a revivified image describing the swift movement of a light boat like the flight of a bird. What has just been said of the imagery is also true of the allusions. The associations with the beautiful Hsi Shih, aroused by the name "Yüeh stream," are greatly reinforced by the "girls washing their silk." We are therefore made to feel that these are beautiful girls, not just common village washerwomen.

Enjambment occurs throughout the poem, so that the rhythm flows freely from line to line. But any danger of becoming formless is averted by the use of antithetical couplets (lines 6 and 7 in stanza 2, and lines 2 and 3 in stanza 3), which, apart from their formalizing effect on the rhythm, also highlight certain points in the description by calling attention to contrasting pairs of images.

No. 13

迎新春

嶰管變青律，帝里陽和新布。晴景回輕煦。慶嘉節、當三五。列華燈、千門萬戶。遍九陌、羅綺香風微度。十里燃絳樹。鰲山聳，喧天簫鼓。

漸天如水，素月當午。香徑裏、絕纓擲果無數。更闌燭影花陰下，少年人、往往奇遇。太平時、朝野多歡，民康阜。隨分良聚。堪對此景，爭忍獨醒歸去。

Ying Hsin-ch'un

Hsieh	*kuan*	*pien*	*ch'ing*	*lü*	
Hsieh	pipe	change	green	pitch	

ti	*li*	*yang*	*ho*		*hsin*	*pu*	*(puo)*
emperor	precinct	*yang*	harmony		new	spread	

ch'ing	*ching*	*hui*	*ch'ing*	*hsü*	*(χiu)*
sunny	scene	return	light	warmth	

ch'ing	*chia*	*chieh*
celebrate	fine	festival

tang	*san-wu*	*(nguo)*
face	three-five	

lieh	*hua*	*teng*
display	flowery	lantern

ch'ien	*men*	*wan*	*hu*	*(γuo)*
thousand	door	myriad	door	

pien	*chiu*	*mo*
all-over	nine	road

lo-yi	*hsiang*	*feng*	*wei*	*tu*	*(d'uo)*
light-silk	perfume	wind	slight	pass	

shih	*li*	*jan*	*chiang*	*shu*	*(żiu)*
ten	*li*	burn	red	tree	

ao	*shan*	*sung*
turtle	hill	high

hsüan	*t'ien*	*hsiao*	*ku*	*(kuo)*
make-noise	sky	flute	drum	

chien	*t'ien*	*ju*	*shui*
gradually	sky	like	water

su	*yüeh*	*tang*	*wu*	*(nguo)*
white	moon	face	zenith	

hsiang	*ching*	*li*
fragrant	path	inside

chüeh	*ying*	*chih*	*kuo*	*wu-shu*	*(siu)*
break	hat-string	throw	fruit	numberless	

keng		*lan*		*chu*	*ying*	*hua*	*yin*	*hsia*
night-watch		decline		candle	shadow	flower	shade	under

	shao-nien	*jen*
	young	man

	wang-wang	*ch'i*		*yü*		*(ngiu)*
	often	extraordinary		encounter		

	t'ai-p'ing	*shih*
	peace	time

ch'ao	*yeh*		*to*	*huan*	*min*	*k'ang*	*fu*
court	country-side		much	joy	people	happy	prosperous

	sui-fen		*liang*	*chü*		*(dz'iu)*
	contented		good	gathering		

	k'an	*tui*	*tz'u*	*ching*
	can	face	this	scene

	cheng	*jen*	*tu*		*hsing*	*kuei-ch'ü*	*(k'iwo)*[17]
	how	bear	alone		sober	return	

The bamboo pipes strike the Vernal Note,
The harmonious spirit of *yang* begins to fill
  the Imperial city,
    And gentle warmth returns to the sunny scene.
             Let us celebrate the festival
             Of the First Full Moon!
             Florid lanterns are displayed
          Over thousands and myriads of doors.
             All over the nine avenues
The wind lightly wafts the perfume from silk dresses.
    The "red trees" are lit up for miles,
             The Turtle Hill stands high,
          And the sky resounds with flutes and drums.

          Gradually, the sky becomes like water,
          As the white moon reaches its zenith.
             On the fragrant paths,
Countless hat strings are broken and fruit thrown.

---

[17]CST, p. 17. For variant readings, see note 19.

As night wears on, in the candles' shades and flowers'
   shadows,
      A young man often
      Has an unexpected adventure.
         In this time of peace,
The Court and the country are full of joys; the people,
   happy and prosperous,
      Gather together in contentment.
      Facing such a scene, how
   Could I bear to go home sober alone?

Notes

St. 1, l. 1. Bamboo pipes. *Hsieh kuan,* literally, "Hsieh pipes,"
alluding to the legend that Ling-lun, by order of the Yellow
Emperor, took bamboos from the Hsieh valley and made them
into the twelve pitch pipes that gave the notes of an octave.

Vernal Note. *Ch'ing-lü,* literally, "Green Pitch," alluding to the
complex system of correspondences according to which the pitch
pipes corresponded to the months and seasons, which in turn
corresponded to the five "elements," the five colors, etc. Since
Spring was supposed to correspond to the color green, the pitch
pipe for the first month, which heralded the arrival of Spring, was
said to have the "green" note.

l. 5. First Full Moon. The original literally has "three-five,"
i.e., "fifteen," meaning the fifteenth of the lunar month, here
understood to refer to the fifteenth of the First Month.

l. 8. Nine avenues. Conventional way of referring to the main
roads of the capital, since the Han capital Ch'ang-an had nine
main roads.

l. 10. Red trees. Apparently a variation of "fiery trees" *(huo
shu),* referring to lanterns hanging from trees or bamboo poles.

l. 11. Turtle Hill. A huge scaffolding on which innumerable
lanterns were placed.[18]

St. 2, l. 4. Hat strings broken. At a banquet held by King
Chuang of Ch'u (seventh century B.C.), the candles went out.
One of the officials took advantage of the momentary darkness to

[18]Meng Yüan-lao, pp. 172-73, 175; Anon. *Hsüan-ho yi-shih,* p. 71. For
similar descriptions of the festival during the Southern Sung, see Gernet,
p. 189.

touch one of the royal concubines, and she broke his hat string (*ying*, a string tied under the chin to fasten the hat) to mark his identity. The King, however, did not wish to punish the offender; so he ordered all those present to break their hat strings. The allusion here simply signifies flirtations in the dark.

Fruit thrown. P'an Yüeh (*ob*. 300) was so handsome that whenever he drove out in his carriage women would throw fruit at him.

Meter[19]

```
        +  +  /  +  -  +  0
     +  +  /  -  -  -  +  a
     -  +  /  -  -  +  a
           +  -  -  0
           -  -  +  a
           +  -  -  0
           -  -  +  +  a
           +  +  +  0
  -  +  /  -  -  -  +  a
  +  +  /  -  +  +  a
           -  -  +  0
           -  -  -  +  a

        +  /  -  -  +  0
        +  +  -  +  a
           -  +  +  0
  +  -  /  +  +  /  -  +  a
-  -  /  +  +  /  -  -  +  0
        +  -  -  0
        +  +  -  +  a
        +  -  -  0
-  +  -  -  /  -  -  +  0
        -  +  -  +  a
        -  +  +  +  0
  -  +  /  +  -  /  -  +  a
```

[19]Cf. TL, 18, p. 6a; TP, 32, p. 17a; TF, 4 *hsia*, p. 136a. The last three lines in all these differ from the CST text, which I have followed. TP wrongly marked the end of stanza 2, line 9, as a rhyme (the character *fu* 莩 has the final *iəu*, which does not belong to the same rhyme category as *uo*). The mistake is perpetuated in TF.

Since the present lyric is the only known example of the meter used, we may assume that Liu Yung invented it for the occasion. The name of the tune, *Ying Hsin-ch'un,* means "welcome the new spring," and is indicative of the nature of the poem itself in this case.

Commentary

In contrast to the three preceding poems, this one is full of the joy of life. Although it may be considered an example of what is known in Chinese as *fen-shih t'ai-p'ing,* which may be freely translated as "painting a rosy picture of peace," the poem is not a perfunctory eulogy but a vivid picture of a gay festival, with all its happy excitement, its colorful pageantry, and the many opportunities it affords for romantic encounters. The Lantern Festival was one of the major festive occasions of the year in Sung times, and during the period when this lyric was written, the celebrations in the capital Pien-liang (modern Kaifeng) went on for five days, from the fourteenth of the First Month to the eighteenth.[20] The veracity of the details in this poem is attested by other contemporary accounts, and it is typical of Liu's realism that he does not refrain from mentioning the amorous activities among the celebrating crowd.

In harmony with the festive occasion described, the language of the poem is relatively formal and erudite, with frequent use of allusions, as pointed out in the notes above. Although this poem is not as good as the previous three, it reveals a totally different world and another aspect of Liu Yung's poetry.

No. 14

菊花新

欲掩香幃論繾綣
先斂雙眉愁夜短
催促少年郎
先去睡鴛衾圖暖

[20]See note 18 above.

須臾放了殘鍼線
脫羅裳恣情無限
　留取帳前燈
時時待看伊嬌面

Chü-hua Hsin

yü	yen	hsiang	wei	lun	ch'ien-ch'üan	(k'iwɒn)
wish	close	perfumed	curtain	speak	stick-together	(love)

hsien	lien	shuang	mei	ch'ou	yeh	tuan	(tuân)
first	gather	two	eyebrow	grieve	night	short	

	ts'ui-ts'u	shao-nien	lang
	urge	young	man

hsien	ch'ü	shui	yüan-ch'in	t'u	nuan	(nuân)
first	go	sleep	mandarin-duck-quilt	plan	warm	

hsü-yü	fang-liao	ts'an	chen-hsien	(siän)
short-while	finish-put-down	remnant	needle-thread	

t'o	lo	shang	tzu	ch'ing	wu-hsien	(ɤǎn)
take-off	silk	skirt	indulge	love	no-end	

	liu-ch'ü	chang-ch'ien	teng
	keep-(suffix)	curtain-front	lamp

shih-shih	tai	k'an	yi	chiao	mien	(miän)[21]
from-time-to-time	about-to	look	her	lovely	face	

Before lowering the perfumed curtain to express her love,
She knits her eyebrows, worried that the night is too short.
　She urges the young lover to go to bed
First, so as to warm up the mandarin-duck quilt.

A moment later she puts down her unfinished needlework,
And removes her silk skirt, to indulge in passion without end.
　Let me keep the lamp before the curtain
That I may look at her lovely face from time to time!

[21]CST, p. 38.

Note

St. 1, l. 4. Mandarin-duck quilt. A brocade quilt with two holes for the necks. A pair of mandarin ducks represent lovers.

Meter[22]

```
+  +  -  -  /  -  +  +  a
∓  +  ±  -  /  ∓  +  +  a
      -  +  +  -  -  0
-  +  +  /  ±  ∓  -  +  a

±  -  ∓  +  /  -  ∓  +  a
±  ∓  -  /  ±  -  -  +  a
      ∓  +  +  -  -  0
∓  ±  +  /  +  -  -  +  a
```

Commentary

This is one of Liu Yung's many lyrics that explore the world of erotic love in a frank and realistic manner, and one in which a shift of attitude takes place from the objective to the subjective. In the first stanza, the poet describes himself in the third person as "the young lover" *(shao-nien lang),* but in the second stanza he speaks in his own person. (Although in the original the first person pronoun is not used, the tone is unmistakably that of the first person, while the woman is referred to by the pronoun *yi.*) Consequently the atmosphere of erotic intimacy is increasingly intensified.

The language of the poem is plain and colloquial for the most part, without any compound imagery or allusions. Enjambment occurs several times, and the syntax is sometimes ambiguous. For example, in the first stanza, lines 3 and 4 could be punctuated either as *"ts'ui-ts'u shao-nien lang hsien ch'ü shui, yüan-ch'in t'u nuan"* ("she urges the young lover to go to sleep first, the mandarin-duck quilt thus made warm"), or as *"ts'ui-ts'u shao-nien lang hsien ch'ü shui yüan-ch'in, t'u nuan"* ("she urges the young lover to go to sleep first in the mandarin-duck quilt, to make it warm.")

[22] TL does not list this meter. TP, 9, p. 25a, has a slightly different reading for the last line. TF, 6 *hsia,* p. 27a, has the same reading as CST, which is based on Chu Tsu-mou, I.

The repetition of the word *hsien* ("first") in lines 2 and 4 does not seem to serve any particular poetic purpose. It is also hard to say what specific effects are produced by the alliterative disyllable *ts'ui-ts'u* (Ancient Chinese *ts'uâi-ts-įwok,* "urge") and the rhyming disyllable *ksü-yü* (A.C. *sįu-įu,* "a moment"). However, the disyllable *ch'ien-chüan* (A.C. *k'iän-k'iwɒn,* "sticking-together, love"), being at once alliterative and rhyming, does seem to reinforce the idea of endless, entangled passion that is suggested by the etymology.

The worlds of Liu Yung's lyrics are all familiar and easily accessible. Broadly speaking, they center round three main themes —homeless wandering, erotic love, and city life. Naturally, these themes are not mutually exclusive and may be seen together. The poems dealing primarily with the first theme often involve verbal landscape painting, but Liu differs from earlier landscape poets like Hsieh Ling-yün (385–433) and Wang Wei (701–761) in that he does not treat Nature as an object of philosophic contemplation or as a source of spiritual comfort, but rather as a backdrop for the drama of human passions. In his poetry, Nature is often seen under the Pathetic Fallacy, colored by the dominating emotion of the speaker, and not as a supremely serene presence indifferent to and unaffected by human emotions. Another feature that distinguishes Liu's poems expressing homesickness from many other Chinese poems on the same theme is that, in the former, homesickness is often mixed with an ardent longing for an absent woman. (See, for example, Nos. 11 and 12.) Although there are thousands of Chinese poems describing a woman's longing for her absent husband or lover, it is rather less common for a Chinese poem to express a man's longing for a woman, especially when the woman is quite openly identified as a singing girl and when there is no possibility that allegory is intended.

This leads us to consider the second kind of world often explored by Liu's lyrics—that of sexual love. It is nothing new to write about love in Chinese poetry, particularly in lyrics, which after all originated as popular love songs; but what is remarkable about Liu Yung's love lyrics is his frank and realistic attitude towards love. Not only is he uninhibited by Confucian puritanism in his descriptions of erotic love, but he is also free from the tendency (common among Western poets) to idealize love or to exaggerate its importance. Sometimes he writes of the pleasures or the pains of love with intensity of feeling and complete candor, as in No. 14 and in the following lines:

> Endless wild desires encouraged by wine—
> This pleasure is getting better and better:
> I'm *entering* paradise.[23]

> How could I, again, as I did before,
> Embrace her fragrance and lean on her warmth,
> Hugging her in sleep even when the sun is high?[24]

> The effect of the wine gets stronger and my
>   amorous thoughts run wild:
> The embroidered mandarin-duck quilt tosses
>   its red waves.[25]

The first quotation above, with its *double entendre* (the original of the second line literally reads, "this pleasure gradually enters a fine scene"), conveys sensuality rather than passion. The second quotation is a passionate cry and reminds one of the anonymous English poet's lines:

> Christ, if my love were in my arms
>   And I in my bed again![26]

The third one is similar to the first in its sensuality, but is more interesting because of the original image it contains—that of the quilt tossing its red waves *(pei fan hung lang),* a conceit worthy of John Donne.

However, at other times Liu treats casual love affairs for what they are, without pretending that they are all-consuming passions:

> After the singing and the feast,
> By chance we shared the mandarin-duck quilt.[27]

---

[23]CST, p. 21.   [26]Quiller-Couch, p. 42.
[24]*Ibid.,* p. 2.   [27]CST, p. 31.
[25]*Ibid.,* p. 25.

I remember the bedroom where we first met;
We should then have stayed together for good.
Who would have thought that a casual tryst
Should turn into the sorrows of separation?[28]

This disarmingly frank attitude, while refreshing in a way, makes the poems appear rather superficial.

A few of Liu's lyrics describe love from the woman's point of view with psychological insight, but others merely paint pictures of attractive courtesans without really showing their feelings.

The third main theme of Liu's poetry is city life—its many splendors and attractions. Again, this is not a new theme in Chinese literature; for instance, writers of "Expositions" (*fu*, also known as "rhymeprose") of earlier periods such as Chang Heng (78–139) and Tso Ssu (250?–305?) wrote long and elaborate descriptions of imperial capitals. But whereas these writers rely for effect on exhaustive catalogues of details, Liu selects only a few. Moreover, while the earlier writers give the impression of being objective if not mechanical in their descriptions of cities, Liu imbues his scenes with emotion, so that the reader feels personally involved. For example, in No. 13 quoted above, we feel as if we were participants of the festival and not mere spectators. It was even said that a lyric by Liu describing the magnificence of Hang-chow so excited the Chin (Juchen) ruler Wan-yen Liang that he resolved to invade the south.[29] Of course we cannot take this story seriously, but it does pay tribute to Liu's power of evoking the atmosphere of a place. The best among his lyrics describing city scenes are comparable to such famous Sung paintings as Chang Tse-tuan's "River Scene during the Bright and Clear Festival" (*Ch'ing-ming shang-ho t'u*) for their realistic depictions of contemporary social life and of scenery.

In short, Liu Yung's poetry is marked by emotional realism, by which I mean that he looks at life in a highly subjective and emotional manner, yet in expressing his subjective emotions he is

---

[28] *Ibid.*, p. 15.
[29] Hu Yün-yi, p. 42; Hsüeh Li-jo, p. 111.

realistic, holding nothing back, assuming no poses, and making no attempt to rise above his emotions. The *persona* that emerges from his poems is a man of normal appetites and tastes, who enjoys with gusto the pleasures of life and suffers with complaint its inevitable hardships, a man who is not ashamed of his all-too-human frailties and who has no higher aspiration than leading a happy life. Liu's sensibility is robust rather than sophisticated, and his ideas are neither original nor profound. However, his emotional realism endows his worlds with truth and saves them (often, though not always) from banality. Since he speaks for the ordinary man rather than the over-refined or the other-worldly, his poetry has a wide and easy appeal. It is not surprising, therefore, that he was the most popular lyricist of his age.

When we turn to Liu's exploration of language, his achievements are seen to be even greater. He was the first to make *abundant* use of colloquial expressions and to blend them successfully with conventional poetic diction, and he made various innovations in syntax, rhythm, and other elements of prosody. Moreover, he was chiefly responsible for the evolution of "slow lyrics" or lyrics in longer meters.

His lyrics are not uniformly colloquial. Generally speaking, colloquialisms occur most often in lyrics dealing with love, less so in those dealing with travel and nostalgia, and least frequently in those describing city life. In all, over a hundred colloquial expressions are found in his lyrics, some recurring with considerable frequency. To give just a few examples, the colloquial pronoun *ni* 你 ("you") occurs eight times and *yi* 伊 ("he" or "she") twenty-nine times. Also frequently used are the colloquial adverbs *jen* 恁 ("thus," fifty times), *cheng* 爭 ("how" in rhetorical questions, eighteen times), and *tsen-sheng* 怎生 (similar in meaning to *cheng*, six times), and the suffixes *cho* 着 (a verbal suffix indicating continuation of action, six times), *erh* 兒 (a diminutive suffix added to nouns, seven times), and *te* 得 (a verbal suffix indicating ability or consequence of action, thirty-six times). Such colloquialisms, when blended with more conventional and elegant diction, add a lively and informal touch to the lyrics, and, when used predominantly in a lyric, give the whole poem a conversational tone.

While Liu Yung is generally successful in his use of colloquial expressions, he does not always show sufficient care in the use of conventional phrases. A certain mental laziness and casualness can be detected in the repeated use of such phrases as *chia-jen* 佳人 ("beautiful person," which occurs ten times), *ti-li* 帝里 ("Imperial city," ten times), and *yüan-pei* 駕被 or *yüan-ch'in* 駕衾 ("mandarin-duck quilt," twenty-two times). These inevitably become tedious after one has encountered them so often.

In his use of allusions Liu also tends to be repetitious, and most of his allusions are practically common idioms. For example, he alludes six times to the beautiful Hsi Shih either by name or as the "maid of Yüeh," four times to Lady Swallow (Chao Fei-yen), three times to the story that women threw fruit at the handsome P'an Yüeh, and twice to the story that Ho Yen had such a fair complexion that he was suspected of using face powder. Such allusions are hardly more than substitutes for "beautiful ladies" and "handsome young men," as the case may be, and do not contribute much to the poetic effect, except when two or more allusions reinforce each other, as in No. 12 above. Again, when he uses a phrase like "Ch'u waists," alluding to the story that a King of Ch'u had such a passion for slender waists that many of his palace ladies starved themselves to death, the expression is only a conventional way of saying "slender waists" and has little to do with the original story about ladies starving themselves. In short, allusions do not play a very important part in Liu Yung's poetic technique; he simply inherited them as part and parcel of conventional literary language.

In his use of imagery, Liu Yung relies considerably on the visual appeal and cumulative effect of simple images, although he also uses compound images with frequency. Among his most frequently used simple images, three groups stand out. First, we constantly encounter such Nature images as mists (by far his greatest favorite), clouds, sunshine (especially the setting sun), moonlight (especially the fading moon), wind, rain, mountains, rivers, and trees (especially willow trees). The general impression created by these images is that of a sweeping misty landscape reminiscent of Chinese landscape painting of the "Southern" school. Here, Nature is not a pleasant garden (as in Yen Shu's lyrics) but an austere setting for the journey of life; one gets the feeling of ever moving against the background of this landscape, with boats sailing, rivers flowing, wind blowing. In contrast to the Nature imagery, the other two groups of Liu's most frequently used simple images concern domestic life and beautiful women. Images like pavilions and chambers, curtains and screens, pillows and quilts, candles and lamps, are used constantly to produce an atmosphere of domestic intimacy, in which the beautiful women dwell. No less constantly appear images that describe their attractions: their eyes, eyebrows, lips, hands, dresses, and ornaments. The three kinds of imagery reflect, on the one hand, the poet's feeling of solitude as he journeys through life in a world that is largely indifferent, and, on the other hand, his longing for happy domesticity and his preoccupation with feminine allure.

Liu's compound images are derived from sources similar to those of his simple images, but they show considerable variety in form and underlying ways of association. Compound images of comparison include some that compare two physical objects, others that compare human beings to natural objects, and still others that compare the mental to the physical or the abstract to the concrete. Examples of the first kind are: "cloudy waves," "fiery clouds," "oily rain," "the sky like water," "the moonlight like water," "the view of the Capital like embroidery," "the view like a painting,"[30] and many others. Images that compare human beings to natural objects include "flower-like girl," "flower-like face," "cloudy hair," "willowy waist," "eyebrows like distant mountains."[31] Images that liken the mental to the physical include the following: "orchid-like nature and fragrant-grass-like heart," "dream following flying catkins and sorrow stronger than fragrant wine," "homeward-bound heart growing wings," and "Even though there is some perfume left, /It too,

[30]CST, pp. 28 (and 41), 54, 40, 17 (and 29), 22, 29, 28.
[31]*Ibid.*, pp. 39, 22 (and 24, 36), 22 (and 53), 24 (and 27), 33 (and 44).

like his love, will fade away day and night."[32]   As is evident even
from this partial list, most of these images are quite hackneyed;
only the last two can claim originality.   However, not all the
familiar images of comparison strike us as being equally banal,
because they often assume different forms.   Some images take the
form of explicit comparisons (or similes), with the use of such
words as *ssu* or *ju,* which correspond to "is like," "looks as if,"
or "resembles" in English.   In addition to the examples already
given, we may cite a few more: "Her lover *is like* (*ssu*) a floating
gossamer that often provokes and entangles her," "The fragrant
grass is green, *as if* (*ju*) dyed," "The waves *seem to be* (*ssu*) dyed,
the mountains *look as if* (*ju*) they were cut with a knife," "Her
talk sounds *like* (*ssu*) a delicate oriole."[33]   These are for the most
part commonplace comparisons.   More original and interesting
are images that effect the comparison by means of stronger verbs
than *ssu* or *ju,* such as: "Her fragrant dimpled cheeks *melt* (*jung*)
融 spring clouds;/Her dark green hair *lets fall* (*to*) 嚲 autumn
mists"; "The candles *light up* (*ts'an*) 爘 numerous stars;/The
incense *draws out* (*ch'ou*) 抽 green threads"; "The leaves *cut*
(with scissors; *chien*) 剪 red silk;/ The chrysanthemums *leave
behind* (*yi*) 遺 golden powder"; and "The waves *toss* (*fan*) 翻
green curtains"[34] (cf. "The mandarin-duck quilt tosses its red
waves" quoted above).   The use of active verbs makes the images
more arresting, even though the underlying comparison may not
be novel.

Images of substitution occur in Liu's lyrics even oftener than
those of comparison.   Most of them are clichés in Chinese poetry,
such as "fragrant cloud" or "green cloud" for a woman's hair,
"autumn waves" for her eyes, and "jade trees and jasper
branches" for her limbs.[35]   Sometimes an image of substitution
may involve an allusion, such as "silver toad"[36] (for the moon),
which alludes to the popular legend that the spirit of the moon

[32] *Ibid.,* pp. 13 (and 27, 36), 16, 22, 46.
[33] *Ibid.,* pp. 46, 38, 41, 15.
[34] *Ibid.,* pp. 44, 19, 15, 45.
[35] *Ibid.,* pp. 13–14 (and 36, 50), 21, 21 (and 25).
[36] *Ibid.,* pp. 16, 38.

assumes the form of a toad. Such substitutions are not very effective either in their imagistic or allusive aspect.

Similar to images of substitution are examples of metonymy ("red" for flowers and "green" for leaves or grass) and synecdoche ("moth-eyebrows" for women). These in themselves are not particularly interesting, but when they are combined with images of transference, they become more striking. For instance, the line "The green decreases and the red is scarce"[37] is not remarkable, but "sad green and grieving red"[38] (which involves the transference of the human attributes "sad" and "grieving" to the green leaves and red flowers) is rather more so, especially since personification is much less common in Chinese poetry than in Western poetry.

Other images of transference include: "The beautiful apricot blossoms *burn* (*shao*) 燒 the woods;/The light-yellow peaches *embroider* (*hsiu*) 繡 the countryside"/; "The morning chill is still *tender* (*nen*) 嫩 "; "Golden strings and jade pipes *choke* (*yeh*) 咽 the spring air"; "The green color *locks* (*so*) 鎖 the window"; "The cold *bullys* (*ch'i*) 欺 the green fields"; "Fading leaves *dance* (*wu*) 舞 in *grieving* (*ch'ou*) 愁 red"; and "The cold stream is *dipped* (*chan*) 蘸 in jade green."[39] Several of these are particularly noteworthy because they involve synaesthesia.

Liu Yung is fond of using two contrasting images in one line, often a tetrasyllabic one, such as:

金波銀漢

chin-po   *yin-han*[40]
gold-wave   silver-river

("Golden wave" is a substitute for moonlight and "silver river" refers to the Milky Way.)

[37] *Ibid.*, pp. 52, 54.
[38] *Ibid.*, p. 29.
[39] *Ibid.*, pp. 48, 15, 20, 46, 13, 54.
[40] *Ibid.*, p. 22.

尤 紅 殢 翠

yu	hung	ti	ts'ui[41]
cling-to	red	linger-over	green

("Red" and "green" here represent gaily dressed women. Several variations of this line occur.)

倚 玉 偎 香

yi	yü	wei	hsiang[42]
lean-on	jade	embrace	fragrance

("Jade" and "fragrance" of course also represent women.)

愁 雲 恨 雨

ch'ou	yün	hen	yü[43]
grieving	cloud	regretful	rain

("Cloud" and "rain" together often signify sexual intercourse, although not always.)

Similarly, two lines each containing an image may be contrasted with each other:

銀 塘 似 染
金 堤 如 繡

yin	t'ang	ssu	jan
silver	pond	seem	dyed

chin	ti	ju	hsiu[44]
gold	embankment	like	embroidery

(The silvery pond seems to be dyed,
The golden embankment looks like embroidery.)

[41] *Ibid.*, p. 39 (also p. 28).
[42] *Ibid.*, p. 24.
[43] *Ibid.*, p. 22 (also pp. 31, 48, 50).
[44] *Ibid.*, p. 16.

柳 抬 烟 眼
花 匀 露 臉

liu   t'ai   yen   yen
willow   raise   smoke   eye

hua   yün   lu   lien[45]
flower   even   dew   face

(The willows lift their smoky eyes,
The flowers smooth their dewy faces.)

層 波 細 剪 明 眸
膩 玉 圓 搓 素 頸

ts'eng   po   hsi   chien   ming   mou
layer   wave fine   cut   bright   pupil

ni   yü   yüan   ts'o   su   ching[46]
smooth   jade round   rub   white   neck

(Her bright eyes: finely cut from layers of ripples;
Her white neck: fashioned from smooth round jade.)

翠 眉 開 嬌 橫 遠 岫
綠 鬢 軃 濃 染 春 烟

ts'ui   mei   k'ai,   chiao   heng   yüan   hsiu
emerald eyebrow   open,   delicate lie   distant peak

lu   pin; tuo,   nung   jan   ch'un   yen[47]
green   hair droop, thick   dye   spring   smoke

(Her greenish eyebrows stretch: distant hills delicately lying;
Her dark hair drooping: thickly dyed by spring mists.)

These examples demonstrate how hackneyed images can be made
more effective by being brought into contrast with each other in
ornately constructed antithetical couplets.

[45] *Ibid.*, p. 19.   [46] *Ibid.*, p. 15.   [47] *Ibid.*, p. 41.

An antithetical couplet is often preceded by an initial monosyllabic segment:

有三秋桂子
十里荷花

yu / *san   ch'iu   kuei   tzu*
have/ three autumn cassia seed

   shih li ho   hua[48]
   ten   *li* lotus flower

(There are the cassia seeds of the three autumn months,
   The lotus flowers extending over ten *li*.)

對雌霓挂雨
雄風拂檻

tui / *tz'u   ni   kua   yü*
face/ female rainbow hang   rain

   hsiung feng   fu   chien[49]
   male   wind   sweep porch

(I face the female rainbow that hangs in the rain,
   The male wind that sweeps over the porch.)

嘆斷蓬難停
暮雲漸杳

t'an/ *tuan   keng nan   t'ing*
sigh/ broken stem hard stop

   mu   yün   chien   miao[50]
   evening cloud gradually distant

(I lament that the broken stem can hardly stop,
   The evening cloud is drifting farther and
     farther away.)

[48] *Ibid.*, p. 39.   [49] *Ibid.*, p. 43.   [50] *Ibid.*, p. 35.

These tetrasyllabic couplets preceded by a monosyllable are the commonest kind. Occasionally we find pentasyllabic or hexa-syllabic ones:

觀露浥縷金衣
葉映如簧語

kuan / lu   shih lü   chin yi
observe/ dew wet   thread gold clothes

  yeh   ying   ju   huang yü[51]
  leaves hide like reed   talk

(Watch the dew wetting the dress threaded with gold,
  The leaves hiding [the oriole that] warbles
    like the reed-pipes.)

會樂府兩籍神仙
梨園四部絃管

hui   / yüeh-fu   liang chi   shen-hsien
assemble/ Music-bureau two   register   immortal

  li-yüan   ssu   pu   hsien kuan[52]
  Pear-garden four section string pipe

(Assembled are the immortals of the two divisions
  of the Music Bureau,
    The four sections of strings and pipes of
      the Pear Garden.)

In rare cases, each line of an antithetical couplet is preceded by a monosyllabic syllable:

見岸花啼露
對堤柳愁烟

[51] Ibid., p. 13.
[52] Ibid., p. 16.

chien/ an   hua   t'i   lu
see / bank flower weep dew

tui / ti   liu   ch'ou yen[53]
face/ embankment willow grieve mist

(I see the flowers on the bank shedding tears of dew;
I face the willows on the embankment grieving
    over the mist.)

對暮山橫翠
襯殘葉飄黃

tui / mu   shan   heng ts'ui
face/ evening mountain lie   green

ch'en / ts'an   yeh   p'iao huang[54]
match/ fading leaves float yellow

(I face the evening mountains lying green,
Matched by the fading leaves drifting, yellow.)

We also find the initial monosyllable introducing three parallel
lines instead of two. One example has been noted before (in
No. 11, stanza 1, lines 3–5), and here are two more examples:

漸素景宸殘
風砧韻響
霜樹紅疏

chien   / su   ching shuai   ts'an
gradually/ pale light decline fade

  feng chen   yün   hsiang
  wind clothes-block harmony sound

  shuang shu   hung shu[55]
  frost   tree red   scarce

[53] *Ibid.*, p. 48.   [55] *Ibid.*, p. 29.
[54] *Ibid.*, p. 48.

(Gradually, the pale light fades away,
The sound of [beating clothes on] the block
  harmonizes with the wind,
The red leaves on the frosty trees become scarce.)

漸亭皋葉下
隴首雲飛
素秋新霽

chien   /   *t'ing-kao*   *yeh*   *hsia*
gradually/ marsh-pavilion leaves fall

   lung-shou *yün*   *fei*
   dike-head   cloud   fly

   su   *ch'iu*   *hsin*   *chi*[56]
   pale   autumn newly   clear

(Gradually, the leaves by the pavilion fall,
The clouds above the fields rise,
The pale autumn air clears up.)

In addition to introducing antithetical couplets and parallel
lines, the monosyllabic segment can of course also introduce
single lines or several non-parallel lines. More than seventy examples can be found in Liu's lyrics. Generally speaking, the
initial monosyllable is a verb, like *nien* 念 ("think of"), *hsiang*
想 ("imagine"), or *t'an* 嘆 ("sigh over"); or an adverb, like
chien 漸 ("gradually") or *keng* 更 ("moreover"); or an adverbial conjunction, like *tsung* 縱 ("even if") or *cheng* 正
("just as").

The use of the initial monosyllabic segment appears to have
originated with Liu Yung and may be considered one of his most
significant contributions to the versification of lyric meters. The
introduction of this initial monosyllable adds to the variety and
flexibility of the syntax and the rhythm, and also increases the
informality of the style.

---

[56] *Ibid.*, p. 47.

When the initial monosyllable functions as an adverb, an inversion of normal word order is involved, for normally in Chinese an adverb precedes the verb but follows the subject, whereas in lines introduced by a monosyllabic adverb, the adverb of course precedes the subject as well (if the subject is mentioned). For instance, the line

漸霜風淒緊

chien	shuang	feng	ch'i	chin
gradually	frost	wind	chilly	hard

from No. 11 would have appeared in prose or earlier poetry as

shuang	feng	chien	ch'i	chin
frost	wind	gradually	chilly	hard

Other kinds of inversion also occur. In the line

雙雙戲鸂鶒鴛鴦

shuang-shuang	hsi,	ch'i-ch'ih	yüan-yang[57]
pair-pair	play	(two kinds of)	mandarin-duck

(Mandarin-ducks play in pairs)

not only is the disyllabic adverb *shuang-shuang* placed before the subject, but also before the verb *hsi*. Even more unusual is the line

漲新萍綠魚躍

chang	hsin	p'ing	lu	yü	yao[58]
swell	new	duckweed	green	fish	leap

with its highly ambiguous syntax. It can be construed in various ways; the best way seems to me to take it as an inversion of

yü	yao	chang	hsin	lu	p'ing
fish	leap	swell	new	green	duckweed

(The fish leap, making the new green duckweed swell.)

[57]*Ibid.*, p. 40.   [58]*Ibid.*, p. 45.

Such inversions constitute further contributions to variations in syntax and rhythm.

Yet another structural feature that affects both syntax and rhythm is enjambment. We have already seen enough examples in the lyrics quoted above, and no more are needed here. Suffice it to say that more than three hundred instances can be seen in Liu Yung's lyrics. Sometimes only two lines are involved, but quite often the meaning runs on through three or more lines. As a result, the verse becomes highly mobile and supple.

By far Liu Yung's greatest contribution to the development of the lyric is his invention of new meters, especially longer ones. His two hundred and twelve extant lyrics involve the use of one hundred and forty-nine meters. (This figure includes variant forms named after the same tune; the total number of tune titles is one hundred and thirty. But since variant forms represent different syllabic and tonal patterns, they should be regarded as different meters.) Of these, one hundred and fifteen appear to be Liu's inventions, or at least new variations on existing meters. Only twenty-seven of the meters used are "little airs" (sixty-two syllables or fewer, the shortest used by Liu consisting of forty-four syllables); the remaining one hundred and twenty-two meters are all "slow lyrics" (sixty-three or more syllables, the longest running to two hundred and twelve syllables).[59] Of course, he did not invent new meters out of the blue, but, being well-versed in music, devised new variations on old tunes, or wrote words for new tunes, or even composed new tunes and wrote words to them. As a result, a large number of new meters were added to the repertoire of the lyric, although many of them have apparently not been used by any other lyricist.

The significance of the "slow lyrics" lies not merely in their greater total length, but also in their greater variety in the length of individual lines and their more widely spaced rhymes. These factors, combined with the use of enjambment, produce greater flexibility in rhythm and make possible a more informal tone.

[59]The shortest is *Su Chung-ch'ing*, the longest *Ch'i-shih*.

Furthermore, these longer meters with flexible rhythmic patterns enable the writer to engage in fairly long descriptions and to introduce movements and transitions not possible in shorter lyrics. Instead of painting brilliant vignettes of life and capturing single moments of perception as the "little airs" do, the "slow lyrics" allow the poet to develop changing moods and record successive impressions. It is no accident that Liu Yung, with his realistic attitude towards life and his expansive mode of expression, should have been the one to develop the "slow lyrics." In general, Liu extended the scope of the lyric both in its exploration of life and its use of language, but he lacks intellectual depth and sophistication, for which he cannot compare with certain other lyricists like Su Shih and Hsin Ch'i-chi.

No. 15   Ch'in Kuan

秦　觀
滿庭芳

山抹微雲
天黏衰草
畫角聲斷譙門
暫停征棹
聊共引離尊
多少蓬萊舊事
空回首烟靄紛紛
斜陽外
寒鴉數點
流水繞孤村

銷魂
當此際
香囊暗解
羅帶輕分
謾嬴得青樓
薄倖名存
此去何時見也
襟袖上空惹啼痕
傷情處
高城望斷
燈火已黃昏

Man-t'ing Fang

shan		mo	wei	yün	
mountain		rub	slight	cloud	

t'ien	nien	shuai	ts'ao	
sky	adhere	withering	grass	

hua	chiao	sheng	tuan	ch'iao-men	(muən)
painted	horn	sound	break	watch-tower	

chan	t'ing	cheng	chao	
temporarily	stop	travelling	oar	

liao	kung	yin	li	tsun	(tsuən)
for-the-time-being	together	draw	farewell	goblet	

tuo-shao	P'eng-lai	chiu	shih	
how-many	P'eng-lai	old	thing	

k'ung	hui	shou	yen-ai	fen-fen	(p'iuən)
vainly	turn-back	head	mist-air	dispersed	

hsia   yang   wai
slanting sun   beyond

han   ya   shu   tien
cold   crow several dot

liu   shui   jao   ku   ts'un   (ts'uən)
flowing   water   surround   solitary village

hsiao-hun   (ɤuən)
melt-soul

tang   tz'u   chi
face   this   moment

hsiang   nang   an   chieh
perfume   bag   secretly   untie

lo   tai   ch'ing   fen   (p'iuən)
silk   girdle lightly part

man   ying-te   ch'ing-lou
merely   win   Green-mansion

po-hsing   ming   ts'un   (dz'uən)
unfeeling   name   exist

tz'u-ch'ü   ho-shih   chien   yeh
this-departure   when   see   (particle)

chin   hsiu   shang   k'ung   je   t'i   hen   (ɤən)
lapel sleeve above   vainly induce   cry   stain

shang-ch'ing   ch'u
hurt-feeling   place

kao   ch'eng   wang   tuan
tall city-wall gaze   break

teng-huo   yi   huang-hun   (χuən)[60]
lamp-fire already   twilight

[60]*Ibid.*, p. 458. For the second character in line 2, CST has *lien* 連 , which I have changed to *nien* 黏 , following Mao Chin's edition (p. 16). See also T'ang Kuei-chang, IV, p. 68. For the third character in line 10, I prefer the reading *shu* 數 to *wan* 萬 . See Mao Chin, *ibid.*, and Jao Tsung-yi, II, p. 66.

Mountains rubbed by light clouds,
Sky adhering to the withered grass,
The painted horn's sound breaks at the watch-tower.
Let me stop my travelling boat
And share a farewell cup with you for a while!
How many past events of Fairyland—
To look back is futile: only scattered mists remain.
Beyond the slanting sun:
A few dots of cold crows,
A river winding round a solitary village.

Soul-searing
Is this moment when
The perfume bag is secretly untied,
The silk girdle lightly torn apart.
All this has merely won me the name
Of a heartless lover in the Green Mansion!
Once gone, when shall I see you again?
In vain have I brought tear-stains to our lapels and
    sleeves!
Where my heart saddens,
The tall city-wall stops my gaze:
The lights are up—it is already dusk.

Meter[61]

```
        ∓  +  -  -  0
        ∓  -  ∓  +  0
   ±  ∓  /  ∓  +  /  -  -  A
        ±  -  ∓  +  0
      ∓  +  /  +  -  -  A
   ±  +  /  ∓  -  /  ∓  +  0
±  -  +  /  ∓  +  -  -  A
        ∓  -  +  0
      ∓  -  ∓  +  0
      ∓  +  +  -  -  A
```

[61] Cf. TL, 13, p. 19b; TP, 24, pp. 3b–4b; TF, 7, p. 38.

```
          -  -  A
        -  +  +  0
     ∓  -  ±  +  0
     ±  +  -  -  A
  +  ∓  ±  ∓  ∓  0
     ±  +  -  -  A
 ±  +  /  ∓  -  /  ±  +  0
∓  ∓  +  /  ∓  +  -  -  A
        -  -  +  0
     ∓  -  ±  +  0
     ∓  +  /  +  -  -  A
```

Commentary

In this lyric, the poet's sorrow at parting from someone he loves, his nostalgia for past happiness, and his regret over the irrevocable passing of time and the inevitability of separation, are all perfectly blended with the external environment to form the poetic world. He first sets the scene effectively by using unusual verbs: the mountains are *rubbed (mo)* by clouds and the sky *adheres (nien)* to the grass, verbs that are colloquial, unexpected, and precise. He then introduces the theme of parting (lines 4–5). Lines 6–8 recall romantic affairs of the past. P'eng-lai, the name of a Taoist paradise (here translated as "Fairyland"), may be used as a poetic euphemism for a house of courtesans, and since the poet uses the more explicit expression "Green Mansion" (cf. No. 5) in the next stanza, it seems reasonable to take P'eng-lai in the same way. It is further possible that the allusion here might refer to a girl whom Ch'in is said to have met while he was staying at a house called P'eng-lai Ke.[62] The "mists" in line 7 seem to have a double function: they represent past events that now appear vague and distant, but at the same time they may also describe the actual scenery. Thus we are imperceptibly brought back to the present. The remaining lines of the first stanza are deservedly famous, for though they are derived from an earlier poem by Emperor Yang of Sui (580–618), they paint a vivid scene and evoke a feeling of desolation, with a few simple images rich in

[62]See Hu Yün-yi, p. 97.

emotional associations.   The setting sun, as often happens in
Chinese poetry, suggests decline, while the "cold" (han) crows
and the "solitary" (ku) village further increase the feeling of
desolation and chilliness.

The second stanza expresses parting sorrow in a more direct
manner.   The syntax of the first four lines is ambiguous.   We can
take the first line as an exclamation, apart from the other lines; or
take the first two lines as one sentence; or take all four as forming
one sentence.   In any case, the lines describe the anguish of the
parting lovers.   "Soul-searing" (hsiao-hun, literally "soul-melting")
is a cliché, but in the present context appropriate enough.   The
"perfume bag" being untied probably refers to a souvenir being
given by one of the lovers to the other. (Men wore perfume bags
too.)   The "silk girdle" being torn apart (fen, which also means
"parting"), as Hu Yün-yi pointed out,[63] symbolizes love, since it
was common for lovers to tie a loveknot, called "same-heart
knot" (t'ung-hsin chieh), with a girdle.   Lines 5–6, derived from
two well-known lines by Tu Mu (803–852), suggest regret as well
as irony: the poet has had no success in his official life, and even
in love he is not credited with sincerity.   Circumstances oblige
him to leave, but the girl thinks he is fickle and heartless.   The
last three lines add a final touch to the landscape and bring the
mood to the verge of despair.   Night has fallen and people in
their homes have lighted their lamps, but the poet has to go,
leaving behind all that he loves in the darkness that his gaze cannot penetrate.

[63] Ibid.

No. 16

望海潮

梅英疏淡
冰澌溶洩
東風暗換年華
金谷俊遊
銅駝巷陌
新晴細履平沙
長記誤隨車
正絮翻蝶舞
芳思交加
柳下桃蹊
亂分春色到人家

西園夜飲鳴笳
有華燈礙月
飛蓋妨花
蘭苑未空
行人漸老
重來是事堪嗟
烟暝酒旗斜
但倚闌極目
時見棲鴉
無奈歸心
暗隨流水到天涯

Wang Hai-ch'ao

mei   ying   shu   tan
plum blossom scattered pale

ping-ssu   jung   hsieh
floating-ice melt ooze

tung feng an   huan   nien-hua   (γwa)
east wind secretly change year-time

Chin-ku   chün yu
Golden Valley fine visit

t'ung-t'o   hsiang-mo
bronza-camel lane-street

hsin ch'ing hsi lü p'ing sha (ṣa)
newly clearing softly tread flat sand

ch'ang chi   wu   sui   ch'e   (tṣ'ịa)
long remember mistakenly follow carriage

cheng hsü fan tieh wu
just-as catkin turn butterfly dance

fang   ssu   chiao-chia (ka)
fragrant thought increase

liu   hsia   t'ao hsi
willow under peach path

luan   fen   ch'un se   tao   jen-chia   (ka)
randomly distribute spring color reach person's-house

Hsi-yüan   yeh yin   ming   chia (ka)
West Garden night drink sound pipe

yu   hua   teng   ai   yüeh
have florid lantern obscure moon

fei   kai   fang   hua   (χwa)
flying canopy hinder flower

lan   yüan   wei   k'ung
orchid park not-yet empty

hsing-jen   chien   lao
travellers gradually old

ch'ung   lai   shih-shih   k'an   chieh   (tsįa)
again   come   everything   worth   sigh

yen   ming   chiu-ch'i   hsia   (zįa)
mist   dusk   wine-banner   slant

tan   yi   lan   chi-mu
only   lean   railing   exhaust-eye

shih   chien   ch'i   ya   (·a)
occasionally   see   nestling   crow

wu-nai   kuei   hsin
cannot-help   return   heart

an   sui   liu   shui   tao   t'ien-ya   (ngai)[64]
secretly   follow   flowing   water   reach   heaven's-end

A few pale plum blossoms remaining,
The floes thawing and oozing—
The east wind has secretly changed the time of year.
To the fine view of Golden Valley,
On the road flanked by bronze camels,
I walk softly on the flat sand when the weather
has cleared.
I well remember following a carriage by mistake,
When catkins were flying, butterflies dancing,
And fragrant thoughts rising fast.
Under the willows, a peach-path
Sent a random share of spring colors to someone's house.

In the West Garden, pipes sounded at a night feast.
There were florid lanterns that obscured the moon,
Flying canopies that hindered the flowers.
The orchid park is not yet empty,
But the wanderer is gradually growing old.
Revisiting the scene, I am moved to sighs by everything.
A tavern's banner aslant in the misty dusk—
I can only lean on the railings and gaze far,
Seeing crows alight now and then.
How could I stop my homeward thoughts
That secretly follow the flowing water to the end of the world?

[64]CST, p. 455.

Notes

St. 1, l. 4. Golden Valley. Chin-ku, name of a private park owned by Shih Ch'ung (249–300), noted for its splendor.

l. 5. Bronze camels. The road outside the palace gate in Lo-yang had bronze camels on both sides.

St. 2, l. 1. West Garden. Possibly referring to an actual garden so-named in Lo-yang, or perhaps used loosely for any fine garden.

l. 4. Orchid park. *Lan-yüan,* either meaning a garden of flowers, or alluding to the Imperial Library, known as Orchid Terrace (Lan-t'ai), where Ch'in Kuan once worked. The former explanation seems better suited to the context.

Meter[65]

```
          -   -   -   +   0
          -   -   -   +   0
    -   -   /   +   +   /   -   -   A
          -   +   +   -   0
          -   -   +   +   0
    -   -   /   +   +   -   -   A
      -   +   /   +   -   -   A
      +   /   +   -   +   +   0
          -   +   -   -   A
          +   +   -   -   0
+   -   /   -   +   /   +   -   -   A

    -   -   /   +   +   /   -   -   A
      +   /   -   -   +   +   0
          -   +   -   -   A
          -   +   +   -   0
          -   -   +   +   0
    -   -   /   +   +   /   -   -   A
      -   +   /   +   -   -   A
      +   /   +   -   +   +   0
          -   +   -   -   A
          -   +   -   -   0
+   -   /   -   +   /   +   -   -   A
```

[65]Cf. TL, 19, p. 3b; TP, 34, p. 19b; TF, 6 *shang,* p. 80b.

Commentary

In some editions, the poem bears the title "Recalling Antiquity at Lo-yang" *(Lo-yang huai-ku)*, but in fact it is not concerned with antiquity but the speaker's own past, especially a past love affair. The poem shifts its focus freely back and forth between present and past. The first six lines describe the present scene. Two telling details—the few remaining plum blossoms and the thawing ice—establish the time of year, which is then made explicit in line 3. Lines 4 and 5, by using the conventional allusions "Golden Valley" and "bronze camels," locate the scene at Lo-yang. Line 6 introduces the presence of the speaker for the first time; line 7 plunges us into the past. The phrase "following a carriage by mistake" is a thinly veiled reference to a romantic adventure, and the amorous atmosphere is intensified by such images as the butterflies, the "fragrant thoughts," the willows, the peach trees, and the "spring colors," all of which are associated in Chinese literature with beautiful women or love. The reminiscence continues in the first three lines of the second stanza; then we are suddenly brought back to the present in the next two lines. In the remaining lines the speaker indulges in nostalgia and melancholy.

The world of the poem is not unusual, but the mode of exploration is interesting, contrasting the present with the past. In particular, the poet observes compelling details, both present and remembered, with a keen eye. Contrasting images are brought into relief by being placed in antithetical couplets: in the first stanza, lines 1-2, 4-5; in the second stanza, lines 2-3, 4-5. Antithesis also occurs within the line: in stanza 1, lines 8 and 10. Finally, the contrast between past and present is highlighted by the parallel structure of the concluding lines of both stanzas and the repetition of the word *tao* ("reach"), as pointed out by the nineteenth-century critic Chou Chi.[66]

[66]Chou Chi, I, p. 24, *mei-p'i* ("eyebrow comment," i.e., comment printed on the top of the page).

No. 17

如夢令

水閉燈被
如深窺侵
沈亭鼠寒寐寐
沈驛破曉無無
夜緊夢送
遙風霜
門外馬嘶人起

Ju-meng Ling

yao	yeh	ch'en-ch'en	ju	shui	(świ)
long	night	deep-deep	like	water	

feng	chin	yi-t'ing	shen	pi	(piei)
wind	hard	post-pavilion	deeply	shut	

	meng	p'o	shu	k'uei	teng
	dream	break	mouse	peep	lamp

shuang	sung	hsiao	han	ch'in	pei	(b'jie̦)
frost	send	dawn	chill	invade	coverlet	

	wu	mei	(mji)
	no	sleep	

	wu	mei	(mji)
	no	sleep	

men	wai	ma	sssu	jen	ch'i	(k'ji)[67]
door	outside	horse	neigh	people	get-up	

The long night is deep, deep, like water.
The wind blows hard; the post-house firmly shut.

[67]CST, p. 462.

Dream broken—a mouse peeps at the lamp.
Frost sends the chill of dawn to invade the coverlet.
　　　　No sleep,
　　　　No sleep!
Outside, horses neigh and people get up.

Meter[68]

```
  Ŧ  +  /  Ŧ  -  /  Ŧ  +  a
  ±  +  /  ±  -  /  Ŧ  +  a
     Ŧ  +  /  +  Ŧ  -  0
  Ŧ  +  /  ±  -  /  Ŧ  +  a
        Ŧ  +  a
        Ŧ  +  a
Ŧ +  /  Ŧ  -  /  Ŧ  +  a
```

Commentary

Without using the usual overtly emotive words like *ch'ou* ("sorrow"), or *hsiang-ssu* ("home thoughts"), the poem succeeds in obliquely revealing the traveller's feelings of loneliness and homesickness by capturing the atmosphere of the deserted post-house on a cold night.

No. 18

河　傳

恨眉醉眼
甚輕輕覷着
神魂迷亂
常記那回
小曲闌干西畔
鬢雲鬆
羅襪剗

[68]Cf. TL, 2, p. 3b; TP, 2, p. 14a; TF, 3, pp. 67a–b.

丁香笑吐嬌無限
語軟聲低
道我何曾慣
雲雨未諧
早被東風吹散
悶損人
天不管

Ho-ch'uan

hen	*mei*	*tsui*	*yen (ngăn)*
plaintive	eyebrow	drunk	eye

shen	*ch'ing-ch'ing*	*ch'ü-cho*
truly	lightly-lightly	peep

shen-hun	*mi-luan*	*(luân)*
spirit-soul	bewilder-confuse	

ch'ang	*chi*	*na*	*hui*
often	remember	that	time

hsiao	*ch'ü*	*lan-kan*	*hsi*	*p'an (b'uân)*
little	winding	railing	west	side

pin-yün	*sung*
hair-cloud	loose

lo	*wa*	*ch'an (ts'ăn)*
silk	stocking	only

ting-hsiang	*hsiao*	*t'u*		*chiao*	*wu-hsien*	*(yǎn)*
lilac	laugh	stick-out		charm	no-end	

	yü	*juan*	*sheng*	*ti*	
	talk	soft	voice	low	

tao	*wo*	*ho-ts'eng*	*kuan*		*(kwan)*
say	I	whenever	used-to		

	yün-yü	*wei*	*hsieh*	
	cloud-rain	not-yet	harmonize	

tsao	*pei*	*tung*	*feng*	*ch'ui*	*san*	*(sân)*
already	by	east	wind	blow	scatter	

	men	*sun*	*jen*	
	depress	hurt	man	

	t'ien	*pu*	*kuan*	*(kuân)*[69]
	heaven	not	care	

> Plaintive eyebrows, intoxicated eyes—
> Truly, when you just take a peep at them,
>   Your soul is bewildered and lost!
>   I remember well that time:
> To the west of the little winding rails,
>   With her cloud-like hair loose,
>   She walked in her silk stockings;

Her lilac of a tongue laughingly put forth, with
endless charm.
>   In a low voice she softly murmured,
>   "When have I ever been used to this?"
>   Before the clouds had produced rain,
> They were blown away by the east wind, all too soon!
>   It hurts you so much,
>   But Heaven doesn't care!

[69]CST, p. 461.

Meter[70]

```
        ±  -  ±  +  a
     +  /  干  -  +  +  0
        -  -  -  +  a
        干  +  +  -  0
  +  +  /  干  -  /  -  +  a
        +  干  -  0
        -  +  +  a
- - /  +  +  /  -  -  +  a
        +  +  -  -  0
     +  +  /  -  -  +  a
        -  +  +  -  0
  +  +  /  -  -  /  -  +  a
        +  ±  -  0
        干  +  +  a
```

Commentary

This is not one of Ch'in's best works, but it is given here as an
example of his daring eroticism and no less daring use of colloquial language. The lyric is not free from clichés—the comparison
of the woman's hair to cloud, the use of "lilac" as a substitute for
"tongue" (a common one in Chinese erotic literature, even
though it may seem offensive or ludicrous to some Western
readers), and the use of "cloud and rain" as a euphemism for
sexual intercourse. On the other hand, there are interesting,
realistic touches, such as the woman's coy denial that she is ac-
customed to amorous encounters, and the speaker's complaint at
the end.

No. 19

好事近

—— 夢中作

[70]Cf. TL, 6, p. 19b; TP, 11, p. 15a; TF, 4 *hsia*, p. 129b.

春路雨添花
花動一山春色
行到小溪深處
有黄鸝千百

飛雲當面化龍蛇
天矯轉空碧
醉臥古藤陰下
了不知南北

Hao-shih Chin

— *meng-chung tso*
    dream-inside written

ch'un lu   yü   t'ien hua
spring road rain add   flower

hua   tung yi   shan ch'un se   (si̯ək)
flower move one hill spring color

hsing tao   hsiao hsi   shen ch'u
walk   reach little stream deep place

    yu   huang-li   ch'ien   po   (pɒk)
    have yellow-oriole thousand hundred

fei yün   tang-mien   hua   lung   she
fly cloud opposite-face transform dragon snake

    yao-chiao chuan k'ung pi   (pi̯äk)
    soar   turn   empty green

tsui wo   ku   t'eng   yin   hsia
drunk lie ancient wisteria shade under

    liao   pu   chih   nan   po   (pək)[71]
    completely not   know   south north

[71]CST, p. 469.

—Written in a dream

By the road in spring, rain has added flowers,
And the flowers have stirred up a hillful of
    spring colors.
I walk to the deep-hidden source of a little stream,
    Where are hundreds and thousands of yellow orioles.

The flying clouds opposite me turn into dragons and snakes,
    Soaring and twisting in the azure air.
Lying drunk under a shady ancient wisteria,
    I cannot tell South from North at all.

Meter[72]

```
    ±  +  /  +  -  -  0
 ∓  +  /  ±  -  /  -  +  a
 ∓  +  /  ±  -  /  ∓  +  0
    +  /  ∓  -  ∓  +  a

∓  -  /  ±  +  /  ∓  -  -  0
    ∓  ∓  /  ±  -  +  a
 ±  +  /  ∓  -  /  ∓  +  0
    +  /  ∓  -  ∓  +  a
```

Commentary

Whether or not this poem was really written in a dream, it does
have a dream-like atmosphere and an ethereal quality. The poet
leads us on, further and further away from the everyday world.
First we follow the road lined with flowers to the hill covered
with flowers; then we follow the little stream to its deep-hidden
source on the hill; now we are high up, facing the dragon-like
clouds; finally we lie down and rest, not knowing or caring which
way is south and which way north.

The language of the poem is as fresh as the scene it describes.
Particularly effective are the unexpected verbs *t'ien* ("add") in
line 1, *tung* ("move" or "stir") in line 2, and *hua* ("turn into,"

[72]Cf. TL, 4, p. 8a; TP, 5, p. 17a; TF, 3, p. 34a.

instead of merely "resemble") in stanza 2, line 1. We may also notice the use of *shan* ("hill") as a "measure word" in *yi-shan ch'un-se* ("a hillful of spring colors") in line 2, and the contrapuntal structure of the first two lines: "spring. . . .flowers/ flowers. . . .spring. . . ."

Ch'in Kuan's poetry presents a limited range of worlds, but he explores them with a greater emotional intensity than Yen Shu and Ou-yang Hsiu, and a more refined sensibility than Liu Yung. In most of his lyrics, the natural world and the human world are inextricably brought together, the former being colored by the dominant emotion of the latter. (However, in one or two lyrics such as No. 19 above, he attains a world that transcends personal emotions.) He observes Nature with a keener eye for detail than Liu Yung, although he seems less responsive to its grandeur. In the realism and frankness with which he expresses emotions, Ch'in resembles Liu, but he is often more subtle. The emotions he expresses are common enough—romantic love, parting sorrow, homesickness; what is uncommon is his combination of emotional intensity with delicacy of feeling, a combination that places him somewhere between Liu Yung on the one hand, and Yen Shu and Ou-yang Hsiu on the other.

In his use of colloquial language, Ch'in is even bolder than Liu, not hesitating to use broad slang at times. However, he tends to keep the two types of language used—the elegant and the colloquial—quite separate, rather than blending them as does Liu Yung. Most of his lyrics are written in the elegant style, but there are some in purely colloquial language, such as No. 18.

In his choice of words, especially when using elegant language, Ch'in shows much greater care than Liu. He is a master of the *mot juste,* the word unexpected but just right. We have seen examples of such words in Nos. 15 and 19 above.

The use of unexpected words often involves imagery of transference, for in applying a word to an object to which it is not literally applicable, the poet is in fact transferring an attribute from an unnamed object to the one being described. For example, when he writes, "The sky *adhering* to the withered grass," in No. 15, he is transferring the attribute of adhesiveness from an unnamed object to the sky. When the attribute transferred is normally a human one, then what is called personification in tranditional Western rhetoric is involved. As I observed before, personification is not common in Chinese poetry in general, but it is quite frequently used in Ch'in's lyrics. Sometimes the personification is barely suggested, as in "rain has *added* flowers" in No. 19, or in "Spring is *growing* old together with the setting sun."[73] Sometimes the personification is quite explicit, as in: "The river moon *knows* that I am thinking of someone far away,/ And comes upstairs to shine on me at twilight"; "In a moment, the *heartless* wind and rain/Have secretly swept the spring colors away"; "After a slight shower, there are peach trees *grieving* and apricot trees *complaining,*/With abundant red *tears*"; "Rain beats on the lotus flowers,—their *tears* will not dry"; and "Holding a cup of wine I urge the cloud to stay a while,/'*I rely on you, cloud, to block Spring's way home.*'"[74] This fondness for personification, apart from the desire for the unexpected word, is also due to Ch'in Kuan's tendency to see Nature under the Pathetic Fallacy: since he imagines that Nature shares human emotions, it is almost inevitable that he should personify natural objects.

His use of other types of imagery is less remarkable. Here are some examples of the more interesting images of comparison: "With myriad dots of red (flowers) flying about, my sorrow is like the sea"; "Spring colors touch you like wine"; "Spring thoughts are like being hit by wine"; "Tender feelings like water, the date of the rendezvous like a dream"; "The freely flying flowers are as light as dreams,/The endless silk-threads of rain as fine as sorrows."[75] The last example is particularly interesting, since it reverses the usual process of comparison by likening the concrete to the abstract, the physical to the mental.

Sometimes Ch'in Kuan takes an image from an earlier poet and

[73]CST, p. 459.
[74]*Ibid.,* pp. 470, 461, 455, 460–61, 460.
[75]*Ibid.,* pp. 460, 462, 457, 459, 461.

develops it further or produces a variation. For instance, his well-known lines

> Even if the whole spring river were made of tears,
>   It could not exhaust in its flow
>   So much sorrow[76]

are derived from Li Yü's even more famous lines

> If you ask, 'How much sorrow can you bear?'
> It is just like a spring river flowing to the east.[77]

Likewise, he took Li Yü's lines

> Parting sorrow is just like the spring grass:
> The longer you walk, the farther you get, the
>   more it grows[78]

and changed them to

> Sorrow is like fragrant grass:
> It flourishes, and grows again after you have
>   uprooted it all.[79]

Such examples show the way in which he succeeded in reinvigorating borrowed imagery. However, he is not entirely free from hackneyed images. (We need hardly repeat the usual list of "cloudy hair," "golden waves," etc.)

In versification, Ch'in Kuan is much less an innovator than Liu Yung. The eighty-four extant lyrics that are undoubtedly by him involve the use of forty-five meters: twenty-six "little airs" and nineteen "slow lyrics." The shortest of these runs to thirty-three syllables; the longest, one hundred and fifteen.[80]   Only three are his original inventions.

In his use of enjambment and the initial monosyllabic segment, Ch'in shows the influence of Liu, although he uses these devices

---

[76] *Ibid.*, p. 458.
[77] Wang Tz'u-ts'ung, p. 9.
[78] *Ibid.*, p. 19.
[79] CST, p. 456.
[80] The shortest meter is *Ju-meng ling*, the longest is *Ch'in-yüan ch'ün*.

less frequently and in a less varied manner. Altogether we encounter over seventy instances of enjambment and forty examples of the initial monosyllable. The latter is generally used to introduce a tetrasyllabic couplet, and occasionally to precede three or even four parallel tetrasyllabic lines.

Ch'in Kuan has been praised very highly by some critics as a great master of the "subtle and concise" (*wan-yüeh*) style, which these critics regard as the "orthodox" style for the lyric.[81] If we discard this preconception of orthodoxy, we must conclude that, exquisite as many of his lyrics are, Ch'in Kuan has not contributed as much as Liu Yung to the development of the lyric as a poetic genre.

[81] See, for example, Cheng Ch'ien, II, pp. 60–61; Chiang Shang-hsien, II, pp. 189–90; T'ang Kuei-chang, IV, pp. 63–65.

CHAPTER 3

Intellectuality and Wit

Su Shih (1037-1101)

One of the most versatile men who ever trod the earth, Su Shih (also known as Su Tung-p'o), poet, essayist, statesman, scholar, calligrapher, and painter,[1] freed the lyric from its supposedly inherent limitations and elevated it to a new level as a serious poetic medium. To him, the lyric was no longer a song form but a literary form, suitable for any theme, from the sublime to the ridiculous. He could write about beautiful girls and gay parties or parting sorrow and homesickness as well as anyone else, but more characteristically he expressed his philosophical views on life and history, thus introducing a strong element of intellectuality, which had hitherto been almost totally lacking in lyrics. Furthermore, he infused many of his lyrics with wit and humor—again, qualities not often seen in previous lyrics. Even when he wrote on romantic love, he could inject a comic spirit into a stereotyped situation. The following are a few of his best and most typical lyrics.

No. 20

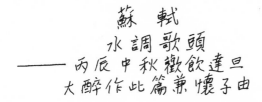

蘇　軾
水調歌頭
——丙辰中秋歡飲達旦
大醉作此篇兼懷子由

---

[1] There is a lively but unreliable biography of Su Shih by Lin Yutang; a brief sketch of Su's life is given in Burton Watson.

明月幾時有，把酒問青天。不知天上宮闕，今夕是何年。我欲乘風歸去，又恐瓊樓玉宇，高處不勝寒。起舞弄清影，何似在人間。

轉朱閣，低綺戶，照無眠。不應有恨，何事長向別時圓。人有悲歡離合，月有陰晴圓缺，此事古難全。但願人長久，千里共嬋娟。

Shui-tiao Ko-t'ou

—*ping-ch'en*	*chung-ch'iu*	*huan*	*yin*	*ta*	*tan*	*ta*
ping-ch'en	mid-autumn	happily	drink	till	dawn	greatly
tsui	*tso*	*tz'u*	*p'ien*	*chien*	*huai*	*Tzu-yu*
drunk	compose	this	piece	also	think-of	Tzu-yu

ming   yüeh   chi-shih   yu
bright moon what-time there-is

pa   chiu   wen   ch'ing t'ien   (t'ien)
hold wine   ask   blue   sky

pu   chih   t'ien-shang   kung-ch'üeh
not   know   heaven-above palace-gate

chin-hsi   shih   ho   nien   (nien)
to-night   be   what year

wo   yü   ch'eng   feng   kuei-ch'ü   (k'i̯wo)
I   wish ride   wind   return

yu   k'ung   ch'iung   lou   yü   yü   (ji̯u)
again afraid jasper   tower jade house

kao-ch'u   pu   sheng   han   (γân)
high-place not   bear   cold

ch'i   wu   nung   ch'ing   ying
rise   dance play   clear   shadow

ho   ssu   tsai jen-chien   (kăn)
how   resemble in   human-world

    chuan   chu   ke
    turn-round   vermilion   chamber

    ti   yi-hu
    lower   carved-window

    chao   wu-mien   (mien)
    shine   no-sleep

  pu   ying   yu   hen
  not   should   have   complaint

ho-shih   ch'ang   hsiang   pieh-shih   yüan   (ji̯wän)
what-for   always   toward   parting-time round

jen	*yu*	*pei*	*huan*	*li*	*ho*	*(γập)*
man	have	sorrow	joy	part	join	

yüeh	*yu*	*yin*	*ch'ing*	*yüan*	*ch'üeh*	*(k'iwät)*
moon	have	cloudy	fair	round	lacking	

tz'u	*shih*	*ku*		*nan*	*ch'üan*	*(dz'iwän)*
this	thing	antiquity		hard	complete	

tan	*yüan*	*jen*	*ch'ang-chiu*
only	wish	man	long-lasting

ch'ien	*li*	*kung*	*ch'an-chüan*	*(·iwän)*[2]
thousand	mile	share	beauty	

—On Mid-autumn of the year *ping-ch'en,* I drank
happily all night and became very intoxicated.
Then I wrote this, while thinking of Tzu-yu.

Since when has the bright moon existed?
Winecup in hand, I ask the blue sky.
I wonder, in the celestial palaces above,
What year it is this very night?
I wish to return there, riding the wind,
But I fear that the jasper towers and jade mansions
Would be too cold, being so high.
As I rise and dance, dallying with my clear shadow,
How can this be the world of men?

It turns round the vermilion chamber,
Lowers itself to the latticed window,
And shines upon the sleepless one.
I should not have any complaints,
But why is it always full just when people are parted?
For men, there are joys and sorrows, partings and reunions;
For the moon, fair and foul weather, waxing and waning:
Things have never been perfect since time began.
I only wish that we should both live long
And share this beauty across a thousand miles!

[2]CST, p. 280.

Notes

Title. Mid-autumn. The fifteenth of the eighth lunar month, one of the greatest festivals of the year. Traditionally this is a time for family reunions. (The term for reunion is *t'uan-yüan,* which literally means "full-round"; hence its association with the full moon.)

Ping-ch'en. The year *ping-ch'en* here corresponds to 1076, when Su Shih was prefect of Mi-chou in modern Shantung province.

Tzu-yu. Courtesy name of the poet's younger brother Su Ch'e, who was then at Tsinan, also in modern Shantung, so the "thousand miles" at the end of the poem is a hyperbole.

Meter[3]

```
    −  +  /  +  −  +  0
    +  +  /  +  −  −  A
 +  −  /  −  +  /  −  +  0
    −  +  /  +  −  −  A
 +  +  /  −  −  /  −  +  b
 +  +  /  −  −  /  +  +  b
    −  +  /  +  −  −  A
 +  +  /  +  −  +  0
    −  +  /  +  −  −  A

          +  −  +  0
          −  +  +  0
          +  −  −  A
          +  −  +  +  0
 −  +  /  −  +  /  +  −  −  A
    −  +  /  −  −  /  −  +  c
 +  +  /  −  −  /  −  +  c
    +  +  /  +  −  −  A
    +  +  /  −  −  +  0
    −  +  /  +  −  −  A
```

Commentary

Let us first deal with a few problems of interpretation and translation before discussing the poem as a whole. The first line

[3]Cf. TL, 14, p. 9b; TP, 23, p. 30b; TF, 2, p. 55b.

has been taken by several previous translators as "When will there be another bright moon?"[4] or "How rare is the moon?"[5] Either interpretation is grammatically possible, but it makes much better sense to take it as "Since when has the moon existed?"[6] for this reading is much more closely related to the question raised in lines 3-4: "What year is it now in heaven?" Both questions implicitly contrast the human perspective of time with the eternity of the universe. Furthermore, as commentators have pointed out, the first two lines of this poem are derived from Li Po's lines, "Since when has there been a moon in the blue sky? I now hold my cup and wish to ask it once."[7] There is an even earlier poem, by Chang Jo-hsü (fl. 711), that contains a similar idea: "By the river, who was the first man to have seen the moon? And in what year did the river moon first shine on a man?"[8] It is clear, therefore, that Su Shih is not wondering how often there is a full moon, but how old the universe is.

Some commentators take lines 5-7 as an indirect reference to Emperor Shen-tsung, citing the story that when the Emperor read these lines he was so touched by the poet's loyalty that he transferred him to a better post.[9] This interpretation is far-fetched, and the unreliability of the story has been demonstrated by Cheng Ch'ien.[10] We should rather take these lines with their references to the celestial palaces as an expression of the Taoist wish for immortality.

Line 9 has been taken to mean, "How can this be like the human world" (i.e., "I feel as if I were no longer in the human world"),[11] or, "How can any place compare with this human world?"[12] The former interpretation is more consistent with the

---

[4]Yu Min-chuan in Payne, p. 272; Liu Wu-chi, p. 111; Alying and Mackintosh, p. 119.

[5]Lin Yutang, p. 175.

[6]Chu Ta-kao in Birch, I, p. 356; CL, Dec. 1962, p. 74.

[7]See Lung Yü-sheng, I, p. 41a; T'ang Kuei-chang, IV, p. 51; Cheng Ch'ien, I, p. 41; Chiang Shang-hsien, II, p. 160; Hu Yün-yi, p. 64.

[8]Chang Jo-hsü, "Ch'un-chiang hua yüeh yeh," CTS, 117, (p. 1,184).

[9]Lung Yü-sheng, I, p. 41b; T'ang Kuei-chang, Chiang Shang-hsien, loc. cit.

[10]Cheng Ch'ien, loc.cit.

[11]Lin Yutang, Ayling and Mackintosh, Birch, loc. cit., T'an Wei, p. 63.

[12]Hu Yün-yi, Liu Wu-chi, CL, loc.cit.

context. Moreover, there is an anecdote recorded by Ts'ai T'ao (early twelfth century), that a singer named Yüan T'ao was once asked by Su Shih to sing this lyric, and, after he had sung it, the poet rose to dance, saying, "To do this *is* to be an immortal!"[13] Since Ts'ai heard this anecdote from Yüan himself, it is probably true. If so, the remark the poet is reported to have made lends further support to the former interpretation.

In the second stanza, *yi-hu* in line 2 does not mean "silk-pad doors"[14] or "gauze window"[15] but a window with elaborately carved latticework comparable to the designs on woven silk. In line 3, *wu-mien* could be "the sleepless one" or "sleepless ones." On the whole it seems better to take it as singular and referring to the poet himself. In line 4, all previous translators have taken the moon to be the implied subject of *pu ying yu hen* ("should not have regret or complaint"),[16] but some commentators think the subject is the poet, and the line means, "I should not have any complaints (since the moon is full)."[17] This is how I have translated the line. In line 7, the phrase *yin ch'ing* means "cloudy or fair" rather than "light and shadow"[18] or "brightness and dimness."[19] In this line, *yin ch'ing* refers to the external circumstances that the moon may encounter, while *yüan ch'üeh* ("waxing and waning") refers to its own mutations, just as in the preceding line the phrase *li ho* ("partings and reunions") represents the external circumstances of human life, while *pei huan* ("sorrows and joys") represents changes in a man's own feelings. In the last line, some scholars take *ch'an-chüan* ("beauty") as an allusion to Ch'ang-o, goddess of the moon.[20] This is hardly necessary, for the word can be applied to the moon itself.[21]

[13] Ts'ai T'ao, *T'ieh-wei-shan ts'ung-t'an,* quoted in Lung Yü-sheng, T'ang Kuei-chang, *loc.cit.*

[14] Payne, Lin Yutang, Liu Wu-chi, *loc.cit.*

[15] CL., *loc.cit.*

[16] Lin Yutang, Liu Wu-chi, CL, Birch, Ayling and Mackintosh, *loc.cit.* Yu (in Payne) is non-committal.

[17] Hu Yün-yi, Chiang Shang-hsien, *loc.cit.*

[18] Liu Wu-chi, *loc.cit.*

[19] Birch, CL, Alying and Mackintosh, *loc.cit.*

[20] Hu Yün-yi, *loc.cit.,* T'an Wei, p. 64.

[21] Cheng Ch'ien, *loc.cit.,* Chiang Shang-hsien, II, p. 161, Hsia Ch'eng-t'ao and Sheng T'ao-ch'ing, p. 79.

So much for the meaning of particular lines. We can now try to follow the development of underlying thoughts throughout the poem. The poet begins by asking how long the moon has existed and what year it is in heaven, thereby making us feel the pathetic brevity and insignificance of human life in contrast to the eternity of the cosmos. He then expresses the Taoist wish to become an immortal by saying that he would like to return to heaven, riding the wind like the legendary Lieh Tzu. Also, by using the word "return," he suggests that he is no common mortal in the first place, but a "banished immortal" like Li Po. However, the poet is skeptical about the possibility of achieving immortality, as shown by the whimsical idea that the heavenly palaces would be too cold for him. Anyway, he continues, it is not really necessary to go to heaven; if one can be spiritually free, this earth becomes heaven. After all, he seems to say, heaven and hell are but states of mind. It is interesting to note that Su Shih, the happy Taoist, says in effect, "Why, this is heaven, nor am I out of it," whereas Christopher Marlowe, the tormented Christian *malgré lui,* makes his Mephistophilis exclaim, "Why this is hell, nor am I out of it."[22]   There could hardly be a more striking contrast between two different attitudes towards life.

The first two lines of the second stanza create a momentary suspense, since we are not sure what the subject of *chuan* ("turn round") and *ti* ("lower") is, until we come to the next line, where the subject of *chao* ("shine"), though still unmentioned, is obviously the moon. These three lines, by describing the moon's shifting positions, imply the passage of time. Night wears on, but the poet is unable to sleep, thinking of his younger brother, to whom he is deeply attached, and regretting that they cannot enjoy the full moon together on this festive night. But he soon reconciles himself to the situation. After all, life cannot always be happy, just as the moon cannot always be full. It is not the nature of things to be perfect. As long as we remain alive and know that those we love share our thoughts and feelings, physical separation does not matter. The poem ends on a note of hope.

Su Shih's amazing imagination and his philosophical mind enabled him to transcend space and time, to roam freely, up to

[22]Marlowe, p. 72.

heaven and back to earth, beyond time and into infinity. As a result, the poem transports us into a world purged of the sordidness and pettiness of the actual world we live in, a world purified and transfigured, yet not without the warmth of human feelings. This is surely one of the most sublime poems ever written in lyric meters.

In spite of its sublime nature, the poem is written in very simple language. Some of the commonest words in the language are used repeatedly: *t'ien* ("sky" or "heaven") twice, *yüeh* ("moon") twice, *yu* ("have" or "there is") three times, *pu* ("not") three times, *jen* ("man" or "human") three times, *shih* ("time") twice, and *shih* ("thing") twice. Yet the language does not give the impression of being monotonous or impoverished, for the ideas the words convey and the powerful rhythm carry us on. Moreover, sometimes a common word is used in an uncommon way. For example, the word *ti* usually means "low," or "to lower," but here (in stanza 2, line 2) it is used in the sense of "lowering itself to," being followed by the phrase *yi-hu* ("latticed window"). This uncommon usage effectively and concisely brings forth the image of the moonlight lowering itself to the window. Apart from this, there are only a few other simple images throughout the poem, such as the jasper towers and jade mansions (which, being descriptions of the celestial palaces, should be taken literally rather than metaphorically) and the vermilion chamber. This sparseness of imagery contributes to the simplicity of the style.

No. 21

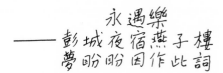

永遇樂
——彭城夜宿燕子樓
夢盼盼因作此詞

明月如霜，好風如水，清景無限。曲港跳魚，圓荷瀉露，寂寞無人見。紞如三鼓，鏗然一葉，黯黯夢雲驚斷。夜茫茫，重尋無處，覺來小園行遍。

天涯倦客，山中歸路，望斷故園心眼。燕子樓空，佳人何在，空鎖樓中燕。古今如夢，何曾夢覺，但有舊歡新怨。異時對，黃樓夜景，為余浩嘆。

Yung-yü Lo

—P'eng-ch'eng yeh su Yen-tzu-lou meng
P'eng-ch'eng night lodge Swallow-pavilion dream

P'an-p'an yin tso tz'u tz'u
P'an-p'an therefore write this lyric

ming yüeh ju shuang
bright moon like frost

hao feng ju shui
good wind like water

ch'ing ching wu hsien (yân)
clear scene no limit

ch'ü kang t'iao yü
winding creek leap fish

yüan ho hsieh lu
round lotus pour dew

chi-mo wu jen chien (kien)
solitude no man see

tan-ju san ku
tan (-suffix) third drum

k'eng-jan yi yeh
k'eng (-suffix) one leaf

an-an meng yün ching tuan (tuân)
dismayed dream cloud startle break

yeh mang-mang
night dim-and-vast

ch'ung hsün wu ch'u
again seek no place

chüeh-lai hsiao yüan hsing pien (pien)
awake (-suffix) little garden walk all-over

t'ien-ya   *chüan*   *k'e*
heaven-end   weary   traveller

shan   *chung*   *kuei*   *lu*
mountain   in   return   road

wang   *tuan*   *ku-yüan*   *hsin*   *yen*   *(ngăn)*
gaze   break   old-garden   heart   eye

Yen-tzu-lou   *k'ung*
Swallow-pavilion   empty

chia-jen   *ho*   *tsai*
beautiful-person   where   at

k'ung   *so*   *lou*   *chung*   *yen*   *('ien)*
for-nothing   lock   pavilion   in   swallow

ku   *chin*   *ju*   *meng*
ancient   modern   like   dream

ho-ts'eng   *meng*   *chiao*
whenever   dream   awake

tan   *yu*   *chiu*   *huan*   *hsin*   *yüan*   *('iwɒn)*
only   have   old   joy   new   grievance

yi   *shih*   *tui*
other   time   face

Huang-lou   *yeh*   *ching*
Yellow-pavilion   night   scene

wei   *yü*   *hao*   *t'an*   *(t'ân)*²³
for   me   great   sigh

—Written after dreaming of P'an-p'an while
staying overnight at the Swallow Pavilion in
P'eng-ch'eng.

²³CST, p. 302.

Bright moon like frost,
Fine breeze like water—
An endless clear view!
In the winding creek fish leap,
Round lotus leaves pour out dew,
All unseen by men in this solitude.
Boom—goes the midnight drum,
Ting—falls a single leaf:
Dismayed, I awake from my amorous dream with
a start.
In the dim, vast night,
Nowhere can I find it again,
As I walk all over the little garden after awaking.

A weary traveller at the world's end,
I gaze at the returning road in the mountains
Till my homeward-bound heart and eyes break.
The Swallow Pavilion stands empty:
Where is the beautiful lady now?
The swallow is locked up inside, all for nothing.
Past and present are like a dream;
Who has ever awoke from the dream?
All we have are old joys and new grievances.
In the future, if someone should face
The night scene at the Yellow Pavilion,
He should heave a long sigh for me!

Notes

Title. P'an-p'an. A beautiful singer and dancer, who was the
favorite concubine of Chang Chien-feng (735-800), military
governor of Hsü-chou (in modern Kiangsu province) during the
T'ang dynasty. He built for her the Swallow Pavilion, where,
after his death, she lived alone for more than a decade, remaining
faithful to his memory.

P'eng-ch'eng. Another name for Hsü-chou, where Su Shih served as prefect in 1078.

St. 1, l. 7. Midnight drum. The original literally says "third drum," referring to the striking of the drum at the third watch, which occurred at midnight.

l. 9. Amorous dream. The original *meng-yün*, literally "dream cloud," is associated with the well-known story that the King of Ch'u dreamed of the amorous Goddess of Mount Wu, who said that she appeared as a cloud in the morning.

St. 2, l. 11. Yellow Pavilion. Built by the poet over the eastern city gate of Hsü-chou.

Meter[24]

```
        ∓  +  -  -  0
        ±  -  ∓  +  0
        ∓  ±  -  +  a
        ±  +  -  -  0
        ∓  -  ±  +  0
     ±  +  /  -  -  +  a
        ±  -  -  +  0
        ∓  -  ±  +  0
  ±  +  /  ∓  -  /  ∓  +  a
        ±  -  -  0
        -  -  ∓  +  0
±  ∓  /  +  -  /  -  +  a

        ∓  -  ∓  +  0
        ∓  ∓  ∓  +  0
  ±  +  /  ∓  -  /  -  +  a
        ∓  +  -  -  0
        ∓  -  ∓  +  0
     ∓  +  /  -  -  +  a
        ∓  -  ∓  +  0
        ∓  ∓  ±  +  0
  ±  +  /  ±  -  /  -  +  a
        ∓  -  ±  0
        ∓  ∓  ±  +  0
        ±  -  +  -  a
```

[24]Cf. TL, 18, p. 11a; TP, 32, p. 20a; TF, 3, p. 36a.

Commentary

This lyric embodies a world of unearthly beauty, in which dream and reality, past and present, romantic fancy and sober thought, reflections on history and personal feelings, are all intermingled. The first six lines evoke a scene of extreme quietness. The images of frost and water produce a chilly atmosphere, while the descriptions of fish leaping in the creek and lotus leaves so heavily laden with dew that they pour it out hint that these natural objects are completely undisturbed by men. This hint is developed into an explicit statement in line 6 ("unseen by men"), which makes us feel as if we were observing the scene not from a human point of view but as it might appear to some visitor from another world, perhaps the ghost of the beautiful P'an-p'an herself. The quietness is shattered by the beating of the drum at midnight, and by the sound of a leaf falling, which, in the stillness of the night, rings out like a bell. The startling effect of these sounds is emphasized by the two onomatopoeic words *tan* (Ancient Chinese *tậm*; here translated as "*boom*") and *k'eng* (A.C. *k'eng*; translated as "*ting*"). The spell is broken, and the poet is aroused from his amorous dream. His dismay and bewilderment as he awakes to face the night are brought out by the reduplicative disyllables *an-an* (A.C. *ăm-ăm*; "dismay") and *mang-mang* (A.C. *mâng-mâng*; "dim and vast").

In the second stanza, his thoughts turn to himself. He is tired of constantly travelling in his official life and longs for his home in southwest China, far away across numerous mountains. The intensity of his homesickness is expressed by the hyperbolic statement in line 3, which in the original has a highly compact and unusual syntax. If put in prose, the line would read something like: *wang ku-yüan erh hsin yen tuan* ("gaze at old garden, and heart and eyes break"). As it stands, *ku-yüan* ("old garden," which stands for "home") modifies *hsin* ("heart") and *yen* ("eye"), both of which are the objects of *wang-tuan* ("gaze-break"), so that the line means, "I gaze till I break my homeward-bound heart and eyes." How much more expressive this is compared with the prose version! But the poet is not merely concerned with his own feelings; he takes a larger view of life and reflects that all human existence is like a dream, no matter how rich, or famous, or beautiful, one may be. Look at this Swallow Pavilion built by a powerful general for his beautiful and talented concubine: it is now empty *(k'ung)*, and the swallow is locked up inside, all for nothing *(k'ung)*. Does this not make one think that all existence is nothingness *(k'ung)*? Yet, such is human nature that, even though we may feel that life is a dream, we cannot really leave this world and cease to have any emotions. So the endless cycle of sorrow and joy goes on, in individual lives as well as in the life of mankind as a whole. Just as he, Su Shih, is now sighing for a long-dead beauty at the Swallow Pavilion built for her, so in the future some yet-unborn stranger would sigh for *him*, at the Yellow Pavilion that he has. built. Truly, as the great calligrapher and poet Wang Hsi-chih (321-79) remarked, "Posterity will look upon us as we now look upon the past."[25] The thought seems both comforting and sad.

The language of this poem is more elegant than that of the previous one. However, common words are not avoided. On the contrary, they are used repeatedly: *ju* ("like") occurs four times, *wu* ("without") three times, *meng* ("dream") three times, *jen* ("man") twice, *k'ung* ("empty" or "for nothing") twice, and *yeh* ("night") twice. These repetitions are not noticeable, since they seem so natural, if not inevitable, in their contexts. The use of parallelism in stanza 1, lines 1-2, 4-5, 7-8, and stanza 2, lines 1-2, adds to the elegance and formality of the style.

No. 22

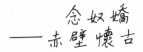

----

[25] *Ch'üan Chin Wen*, 26, p. 10a, in Yen K'e-chün.

大江東去
浪淘盡
千古風流人物
故壘西邊人道是
三國周郎赤壁
亂石穿空
驚濤拍岸
捲起千堆雪
江山如畫
一時多少豪傑

遙想公瑾當年
小喬初嫁了
雄姿英發
羽扇綸巾談笑間
強虜灰飛烟滅
故國神遊
多情應笑我
早生華髮
人生如夢
一尊還酹江月

Nien-nu Chiao

—*Ch'ih-pi   huai-ku*
Red-cliff   recall-antiquity

Ta-chiang   *tung*   *ch'ü*
Great-river   east   depart

     lang   *t'ao*   *chin*
     wave   wash   exhaust

ch'ien-ku   *feng-liu*   *jen-wu*   *(wįuət)*
thousand-age   wind-flow   human-character

ku   *lei*   *hsi-pien*   *jen*   *tao*   *shih*
old   rampart   west-side   people   say   be

San-kuo   *Chou*   *lang*   *Ch'ih-pi*   *(piek)*
Three-kingdom   Chou   young-man   Red-cliff

     luan   *shih*   *ch'uan*   *k'ung*
     disorderly   rock   pierce   air

     ching   *t'ao*   *p'o*   *an*
     startle   billow   slap   bank

     chüan   *ch'i*   *ch'ien*   *tui*   *hsüeh*   *(sįwät)*
     roll   up   thousand   heap   snow

     chiang   *shan*   *ju*   *hua*
     river   mountain   like   picture

yi-shih   *to-shao*   *hao-chieh*   *(g'įät)*
one-time   how-many   hero

     yao   *hsiang*   *Kung-chin*   *tang-nien*
     distant   imagine   Kung-chin   that-year

     Hsiao   *Ch'iao*   *ch'u*   *chia*   *liao*
     Little   Ch'iao   first   marry   (suffix)

     hsiung   *tzu*   *ying-fa*   *(pįwɒt)*
     manly   air   brilliant

yü   *shan*   *kuan*   *chin*   *t'an*   *hsiao*   *chien*
feather   fan   silk   turban   talk   laughter   amidst

     ch'iang   *lu*   *hui*   *fei*   *yen*   *mieh*   *(mįät)*
     powerful   enemy   ash   fly   smoke   vanish

ku   kuo   shen   yu
old   kingdom   spirit wander

to-ch'ing   ying   hsiao   wo
much-feeling should laugh   me

tsao   sheng   hua-fa   (piwɒt)
early   grow   grey-hair

jen-sheng   ju   meng
human-life   like dream

yi-tsun   huan lei   chiang yüeh   (ngiwɒt)[26]
one-goblet   still pour-libation river   moon

—Recalling Antiquity at Red Cliff

The Great River flows to the east:
  Its waves have washed away
All the men of untrammeled spirit of a thousand ages.
To the west of the ancient ramparts, they say,
Is the Red Cliff of young Chou of the Three Kingdoms.
  Random rocks pierce the air,
  Startling billows slap the banks,
Rolling up a thousand heaps of snow.
  The river and the mountains are like a picture—
At one time, how many heroes were there!

Imagine Lord Chou as he was, so long ago,
  When the Younger Ch'iao had just married him:
  His brilliant wit and manly air!
Feather fan in hand, silk-turbaned, amid talk and laughter
He turned the powerful enemy into flying ashes
  and vanishing smoke.

[26]CST, p. 282. There are several variant readings in other editions. I
have followed CST except for the penultimate line, where CST has
jen-chien 人 閒 instead of jen-sheng 人 生, the reading I prefer, following
Wang Yi-ch'ing, I, 70, pp. 1a–b.

> As my spirit wanders to the ancient kingdom,
> You may well laugh at me for being so sentimental
> And growing grey hair so soon!
> Man's life is like a dream—
> Still, let me pour a libation to the river moon!

Notes

Title. In A.D. 208, Chou Yü (175–210), Commander-in-Chief of Wu, defeated the overwhelming forces of Ts'ao Ts'ao and destroyed the latter's mighty fleet by fire at Red Cliff (Ch'ih-pi). Actually, there are four places so called, all in modern Hupeh province.[27] The Red Cliff where the famous battle was fought is near Chia-yü district, whereas the one visited by the poet when he wrote this poem is near Huang-chou (where he lived as a demoted and banished official from 1080 to 1084). The poet himself was not sure about the location of the battle, but since he was concerned only with expressing his thoughts inspired by the historical event associated with the name Red Cliff, the geographical inaccuracy is of no consequence.

St. 1, l. 1. Great River. The Yangtze.

l. 3. Untrammeled spirit. The original expression is *feng-liu,* literally "wind-flow," a term that was at first used to describe men of free spirit and unrestrained behavior, but later, in popular usage, came to mean "dandyish," "gay" (not in the current sense), or even "licentious." The poet here is of course using it in the earlier sense; hence I have translated it this way. Cf. Irving Lo, *Hsin Ch'i-chi,* pp. 3–9, 144n.

l. 5. Young Chou. Chou Yü was known as "Chou *lang*" because of his youth, *lang* being a familiar way of addressing or referring to a young man.

Three Kingdoms. Strictly speaking, at the time the famous battle was fought, the Three Kingdoms (Wei, Shu, and Wu) had not yet formally come into being. Ts'ao Ts'ao, the actual founder of Wei, never assumed the imperial title but remained nominally Prime Minister of the moribund Han dynasty, while Chou Yü was serving under Sun Ch'üan, Marquis of Wu.

[27]Cheng Ch'ien, I, p. 43; Chiang Shang-hsien, II, p. 163.

St. 2, l. 1. Lord Chou. The original has "Kung-chin," Chou Yü's courtesy name. I have changed it to "Lord Chou" for easier identification.

l. 2. Younger Ch'iao. The younger of two sisters of the Ch'iao family, both famous beauties. The elder one married Sun Ts'e, elder brother of Sun Ch'üan.

l. 3. Brilliant wit. The original is *ying-fa,* which can be taken to mean "heroically shining forth," but, as some editors pointed out,[28] the phrase was used by Sun Ch'üan in discussing another general who, he said, could not compare with Chou Yü for his *ying-fa* in discussion. Hu Yün-yi therefore explained the expression as "outstanding in discussion and opinions."[29] However, it seems to me the term itself need not imply "discussion," although it was used with reference to it. I have therefore translated it by the more general phrase "brilliant wit."

l. 4. Feather fan and silk turban. Traditional accoutrement for a scholar at ease.

l. 7. Sentimental. The original is *to-ch'ing,* literally "much-feeling," which can mean "loving," "affectionate," or "sentimental." The syntax of this line is ambiguous and will be discussed further in the commentary below.

Meter[30]

```
          +  -  -  +   0
             +  -  +   0
    -  +  /  -  -  /  -  +  a
 +  +  -  -  /  -  +  +   0
    -  +  /  -  -  /  +  +  a
       +  +  -  -   0
       -  -  +  +   0
    +  +  /  -  +  +  a
       -  -  -  +   0
    +  -  /  -  +  /  -  +  a
```

[28]Lung Yü-sheng, 2, p. 106.
[29]Hu Yün-yi, p. 76.
[30]Cf. TL, 16, p. 7b; TP, 28, p. 8a; TF, 4 *hsia,* p. 34b. These differ from one another in punctuation and line-divisions. The metrical diagram given is in accordance with the text as I have arranged it.

```
        -  +  /  -  +  -  -  0
           +  -  /  -  +  +  0
              -  -  /  -  +  a
     +  +  -  -  /  -  +  -  0
        -  +  /  -  -  -  /  -  +  a
           +  +  -  -  0
              -  -  /  -  +  +  0
              +  -  -  +  a
              -  -  -  +  0
     +  -  /  -  +  /  -  +  a
```

Commentary

This poem offers a heroic and tragic vision of history, against the background of the majesty of Nature. In the first three lines, the great river is a symbol of the passing of time. At the same time, paradoxically, the river also represents the abiding features of Nature, in contrast to the transciency of human life and history: dynasties come and go, but the river remains forever. In the ensuing lines of the first stanza, the poet continues to juxtapose human history with Nature's permanency. Lines 4–5 recall past history, while lines 6–9 present the natural scenery as it is, and was centuries ago, and presumably will be in the future. Line 10 abruptly harks back to the past, emphasizing the contrast between the natural scene and the historical episode that, in human terms, is a momentous event, but, against the eternity of Nature, pales in significance. Such is the tragic fate of all heroic men and deeds!

In the second stanza, the first five lines paint an imaginary portrait of the hero Chou Yü—young, brilliant, handsome, cultured, a lover of beauty and a great strategist who, faced with a powerful enemy, never lost his "cool" but won a famous victory almost casually. Here was a man indeed! Where is he now? And what about the poet himself, middle-aged, exiled, and frustrated in his ambitions? But how silly and sentimental to get all worked up about something that happened so long ago! No wonder he is turning grey so early in life! It is the common lot of all men to be washed away by the flow of time, so why not try to console oneself with wine and the beauties of Nature?

The poem is written in a simple and straightforward style, with occasional touches of colloquialisms like *jen tao shih* ("people say it is") and *ch'u chia liao* ("just got married"). Once more, we find the repeated use of ordinary words: *chiang* ("river") three times, *ch'ien* ("thousand") twice, *ku* ("ancient") twice, *jen* ("man") three times, *kuo* ("kingdom") twice, and *ju* ("like") twice. These do not attract undue attention but seem inevitable where they occur. The language of the poem is not highly allusive. Although in the first three lines there may be echoes of Confucius and of Li Po, as C. N. Tay pointed out,[31] these are not intended as specific allusions. As for the allusions to Chou Yü and his wife and to the battle of Red Cliff, they are so well known that no Chinese reader would fail to recognize them.

The imagery is powerful rather than elaborate. In the first stanza, images of transference are present when the waves are said to have "washed" away all the men of untrammeled spirit of the past, the rocks to "pierce" the air, and the billows to "slap" the banks and "roll up" heaps of snow. The use of these verbs creates an impression of terrific force and movement, an impression further enhanced by the substitution, "thousand heaps of snow," for "foams." In the second stanza, the simple images, "feather fan" and "silk turban" (*yü-shan kuan-chin*), form a sharp contrast to the compound images of comparison, "fly [like] ashes and vanish [like] smoke" (*hui-fei yen-mieh*), thus setting off Chou Yü's ease and composure against his enemy's plight. The latter two images are derived from a Buddhist sutra[32] and may further suggest the illusory nature of all human glory, but their primary function is undoubtedly to describe the annihilation of the enemy fleet by fire.

The poem shows some syntactic flexibility and ambiguity. For instance, lines 7-8 in the second stanza, *to-ch'ing ying hsiao wo, tsao sheng hua-fa*, can be construed as an inversion of *ying hsiao wo to-ch'ing, tsao sheng hua-fa*, meaning "[People] should laugh at me for being so sentimental and growing grey hair so soon." This is how I have translated the lines. But some commentators

[31] C. N. Tay, p. 295.
[32] *Ibid.*, n. 56; Lung Yü-sheng, 2, p. 10b.

prefer to take *to-ch'ing* as "the affectionate one" and as the subject of "should laugh"; the lines would then mean, "The affectionate one should laugh at me for growing grey hair so soon." These commentators further identify the "affectionate one" either with the poet's deceased wife,[33] or with the hero Chou Yü.[34] The former identification is farfetched, for remembrance of the poet's deceased wife would not be particularly relevant to the general theme and tone of the poem. The latter identification also seems unnecessary, for the contrast between the successful young hero and the frustrated middle-aged poet is clear enough without making the hero laugh at the poet.

The flexibility of Su Shih's syntax, together with his free use of enjambment, contributes to the uninterrupted flow of the powerful rhythm. His apparent disregard for conventional line divisions has caused great trouble to prosodists and editors. For instance, in the second stanza, most other lyricists would have four syllables in the second line and five in the third, but in the present poem the words *Hsiao Ch'iao ch'u chia liao* ("The Younger Ch'iao had just got married") clearly form one line, and it is absurd to take the suffix *liao* as the beginning of the next line, as some insist.[35] The truth is that Su Shih would not allow metrical niceties to hamper the expression of his mind, but would vary the syntax and the rhythm according to the drift of his thought.

Yet it would be wrong to think that he was completely indifferent or insensitive to the auditory effects of words. C. N. Tay has ingeniously remarked that the first two lines of this poem, with their succession of "open-throat" vowels and their alternation of Falling and Level Tones, suggest "solemn goose-stepping to rolling drums" and "the roar of the river rolling

[33] Cheng Ch'ien, I, p. 43.

[34] T'an Wei, p. 66.

[35] TP, *loc.cit.;* Chu Yi-tsun, 6, p. 3a; refuted by Ting Shao-yi, 13, p. 6b (quoted in Chiang Shang-hsien, II, p. 164).

forever on."[36]   However, we should remember that although the auditory effects can reinforce the imagery, they cannot by themselves engender any particular images. A succession of certain vowels and of certain kinds of tones, without any meaning attached, would not automatically suggest a military march, or a river rolling on, or anything else. It is only when sound, meaning, and imagery all enrich each other that the fullest poetic effect is produced.

No. 23

水龍吟
—— 次韻章質夫楊花詞

似花還似非花
也無人惜從教墜
拋家傍路
思量卻是
無情有思
縈損柔腸
困酣嬌眼
欲開還閉
夢隨風萬里
尋郎去處
又還被鶯呼起

[36]C. N. Tay, p. 294.

不恨此花飛盡
恨西園
落紅難綴
曉來雨過
遺蹤何在
一池萍碎
春色三分
二分塵土
一分流水
細看來
不是楊花
點點是離人淚

Shui-lung Yin

—tz'u-yün	Chang	Chih-fu	yang-hua		tz'u
follow-rhyme	Chang	Chih-fu	willow-flower		lyric

ssu	hua	huan	ssu	fei	hua
seem	flower	yet	seem	not	flower

yeh	wu-jen	hsi	ts'ung-chiao	chui	(d'wi)
also	no-person	pity	allow-let	fall	

p'ao	chia	pang	lu
desert	home	beside	road

ssu-liang	ch'üeh	shih
think-ponder	however	be

wu	ch'ing	yu	ssu	(si)
not-have	feeling	have	thought	

yung	sun	jou	ch'ang
entwine	hurt	soft	intestine

k'un	han	chiao	yen
sleepy	deep	delicate	eye

yü   k'ai   huan   pi   (piei)
about-to   open   yet   close

meng   sui   feng   wan   li
dream follow wind   ten-thousand   li

hsün   lang   ch'ü-ch'u
seek   lover depart-place

yu   huan   pei   ying   hu   ch'i   (kji)
again   yet   by   oriole   cry   rise

pu   hen   tz'u   hua   fei   chin
not   grieve   this   flower   fly   exhaust

hen   hsi   yüan
grieve   west   garden

lo   hung   nan   chui   (t̂iwäi)
fallen   red   hard   gather

hsiao-lai   yü   kuo
dawn-come   rain   over

yi-tsung   ho-tsai
left-trace   where-at

yi   ch'ih   p'ing   sui   (suâi)
one   pond   duckweed   broken

ch'un   se   san   fen
spring color   three   part

erh   fen   ch'en-t'u
two   part   dust-earth

yi   fen   liu-shui   (świ)
one   part   flow-water

hsi   k'an-lai
close   look (suffix)

pu   shih   yang-hua
not   be   willow-flower

tien-tien   shih   li-jen   lei   (ljwi)[37]
drop-drop   be   parted-person   tear

[37]CST, p. 277.

—After Chang Chih-fu's lyric on the willow catkin,
using the same rhyming words.

It seems to be a flower, yet not a flower,
And no one shows it any pity: let it fall!
     Deserting home, it wanders by the road;
     When you come to think of it, it must
     Have thoughts, insentient as it may be.
     Its tender heart twisted by grief,
     Its delicate eyes heavy with sleep,
     About to open, yet closed again.
   In its dream it follows the wind for ten thousand miles,
     To find where its lover has gone,
But then it is aroused by the oriole's cry once more.

I do not grieve that the willow catkins have all flown away,
     But that, in the Western Garden,
     The fallen red cannot be gathered.
     When dawn comes and the rain is over,
     Where are the traces they have left?
     A pond full of broken duckweeds!
     Of all the colors of springtime,
     Two-thirds have gone with the dust,
     And one-third with the flowing water!
     When you look closely,
     These are not willow catkins,
But, drop after drop, parted lovers' tears!

Notes

Title. Chang Chih-fu is the courtesy name of Chang Chieh, a friend and colleague of Su Shih's. It was a common practice to write a poem to "harmonize" (*ho*) with another one written by someone else, and if one used the same rhyming words as in the original poem, this was called "following the rhymes" (*tz'u-yün*). This poem was written in 1087.

St. 2, l. 2. Western Garden. See note on No. 16, St. 2, l. 1.

l. 6. Duckweeds. Su Shih's own note reads, "It is said that when willow catkins fall into the water, they turn into duckweeds. I have tested it and found it true."

Meter[38]

```
  ±  -  /  ∓  +  /  -  -  0
±  -  ±  +  /  -  -  +  a
      ∓  -  ±  +  0
      -  -  ±  +  0
      ∓  -  ∓  +  a
      ±  +  -  -  0
      ±  -  -  +  0
      ±  -  -  +  a
   +  ∓  -  ±  +  0
      ∓  -  ±  +  0
   ∓  ∓  +  /  -  -  +  a
   ±  +  /  ∓  -  /  ∓  +  0
         +  -  -  0
      ∓  -  -  +  a
      ∓  -  +  +  0
      ∓  -  ∓  +  0
      ±  -  ±  +  a
      ∓  +  -  -  0
      ∓  +  -  -  0
      ±  -  -  +  a
         +  -  -  0
      ±  +  -  -  0
   ∓  +  +  /  -  -  +  a
```

This meter has a number of variations, and editors and prosodists differ with regard to the line divisions of the present lyric. In the first stanza, the last line could be divided into two lines. In the second stanza, what I have given as lines 2 and 3 above could be considered one line, with a pause after the third syllable. The same applies to lines 10 and 11. Furthermore, some prefer to punctuate the last three lines thus:

> *hsi   k'an-lai*
> *pu   shih   yang-hua   tien-tien*
> *shih   li-jen   lei*

[38]Cf. TL, 16, pp. 18b–19a; TP, 30, p. 13b; TF, 2, p. 60a. These differ from one another in line-divisions.

(When you look closely,
　They are not willow catkins, drop after drop;
　　They are parted lovers' tears.)

According to this punctuation, the tone pattern of these lines
would be:

```
  ˘  +  -  -
+  +  /  -  -  +  +
   +  -  -  +
```

Still others would have these lines punctuated this way:

hsi k'an-lai pu shih
　yang-hua tien-tien
　shih li-jen lei

(When you look closely, they are not
　Willow catkins, drop after drop;
　　They are parted lovers' tears.)

The tone pattern would then become:

```
+  -  -  +  +
   -  -  +  +
   +  -  -  +
```

Commentary

　It is difficult to imagine a more striking example of how genius
triumphs over technical restraints.　When a poet is faced with the
task of writing a poem on a given subject (and a seemingly trivial
one at that) and of using the same meter and the same rhyming
words as an existing poem, one may well expect the result to be
highly contrived and unconvincing.　Yet under these circumstances Su Shih produced an original poem that does not sound
at all forced.　It is as if someone had written another "Ode to a
Nightingale" using the same meter and rhyming words as Keats
yet successfully expressing his own thoughts and feelings.　Moreover, the poem transforms description of a minute object into
a symbolic embodiment of various kinds of imagined emotional
experiences.　This is accomplished with the help of paradoxes,
imagery, and other poetic devices.

The very first line of the poem (possibly derived from Po Chü-yi's "Flower, yet not flower") is a paradox, which points out the ambiguous character of the willow catkin and poses the question whether or not it is a flower. Then, in line 3, the catkin is implicitly compared to a homeless wanderer. Once this personification is introduced, the catkin can naturally be supposed to have thoughts of its own, but instead of attributing thoughts to it in a forthright manner, Su uses another paradox in line 5, which literally runs, "have no feeling but have thoughts." In the remaining lines of the first stanza, the personification continues but with a different vehicle: the catkin is now compared to a beautiful woman lying in sorrowful sleep. This change of vehicle is not noticeable in the original because the subjects of the verbs are not mentioned. The imagery in lines 6–8 can be interpreted in different ways. Hu Yün-yi takes *jou-ch'ang* (literally "soft intestines," translated here as "tender heart," since in Chinese one breaks one's "intestines" instead of "heart") as a description of willow twigs, and *chiao-yen* ("delicate eyes") as one of young leaves.[39] This would damage the consistency of the imagery by shifting attention from the catkin to the willow tree. I prefer, therefore, to take both images as referring to the catkin itself: the former comparing the seed surrounded by twisting downs to a woman's heart surrounded by lingering sorrow, and the latter comparing the twinkling light on the catkins to the blinking of drowsy eyes. By means of these fantastic images, the poet evokes the picture of a sleeping woman, who is then imagined to be dreaming of her lover far away. We have now left the world of physical objects far behind and entered that of human emotions, albeit purely imaginary ones. The last line of the first stanza contains an echo of a famous quatrain by the T'ang poet Chin Ch'ang-hsü:

Chase away that yellow oriole,
Don't let it cry on the twig,
For when it cries, it arouses me from
   my dream,
And I shall not be able to reach Liao-hsi.[40]

[39] Hu Yün-yi, p. 85.
[40] CTS, 768 (p. 8,724).

Inside the wall, a garden swing; outside the wall, a road.
Outside the wall, a passer-by,
Inside the wall, a pretty girl's laughter.
Gradually, the laughter is heard no more, the sound
dies away,
And the one who is all heart is angered by the heartless
one!

Meter

See No. 2.

Commentary

The first stanza paints a delightful scene of late spring with a few deft strokes, and the second presents a comedy in miniature. The romantic situation, which in the hands of another writer could easily have been sentimentalized, is here observed with good-natured humor. The sense of fun is evoked by the witty juggling of such simple words as *ch'iang* ("wall"), *jen* ("person"), and *hsiao* ("laugh"). Some commentators think that "the one who is all heart" (*to-ch'ing,* literally "one who has much feeling") refers to the passer-by and the "heartless one" (*wu-ch'ing,* or "one who has no feelings") refers to the girl.[42] I would prefer to take it the other way round: as the passer-by leaves, the girl becomes angry with him for not staying longer.

It is surely unnecessary to take, as Hu Yün-yi does, the passer-by as the poet himself, and the poem as an expression of his feeling of disappointment while in exile.[43]

Su Shih has often been called the founder of the "powerful and free" (*hao-fang*) school of the lyric, but this description does scant justice to the scope and variety of his lyrics, which explore different worlds in different styles. His worlds can be sublime and transcendental (as in No. 20), or cold and eerie (as in No. 21), or heroic and tragic (as in No. 22), or delicate and dreamlike (as in No. 23), or lively and gay (as in No. 24). Externally, his lyrics reflect both the natural world and the human world, often jux-

[42] Hu Yün-yi, p. 88.   [43] *Ibid.,* p. 89.

taposing the two. Nature in all its splendor is sometimes seen as a symbol of eternity in contrast to human existence, and sometimes as a source of sensuous enjoyment or spiritual solace. Both these attitudes to Nature are quite common in Chinese poetry. However, what is remarkable about some of Su's lyrics (such as Nos. 21 and 22) is that they not only contrast the eternity of Nature with the transiency of individual human life but also introduce a third element: history. In these lyrics, the poet's personal life is measured against the span of history, which in turn is measured against the infinity of the universe, so that three different perspectives of time—personal, historical, and cosmic— are presented. I believe that Su was the first poet to exploit this triple perspective in lyrics, though earlier examples can be found in the verse (shih) of Li Po, Tu Fu, and others.

With regard to inner experiences, Su's lyrics also exhibit great variety. Apart from philosophical reflections and whimsical fancies, they cover a wide range of emotions, from tender conjugal love and deep fraternal affection to lighthearted admiration for pretty singing girls, and from moods of solitude and frustration to those of conviviality and exhaltation. Unlike most other lyricists, he is rarely lachrymose or mawkish, but often transcends his emotions and accepts his situation with stoic calm or gentle self-mockery. A pervading intellect and a sparkling wit are his hallmarks. Even when he writes on such an unpromising subject as taking a bath, this mundane activity is treated, in a half-humorous manner, as a Buddhist symbol of spiritual purification.[44]

Stylistically, Su's lyrics show three types of diction—the colloquial, the elegant, and the erudite. In his use of colloquial language, he was probably influenced by Liu Yung, although he affected to despise the latter's works. As a matter of fact, almost as many colloquialisms are found in Su's lyrics as in Liu's. Among the numerous colloquial expressions used by him, a random sampling may be offered: nouns like lao-p'o 老婆 ("old woman"); pronouns like nung 儂 (first person), ni 你 (second person), and yi 伊 (third person); verbs like t'ou-yen 偷眼

[44]CST, p. 311.

("steal a look at"), *mao-tsao* 眊矂 ("feel depressed"), *k'ai* 揩 ("wipe"), *nien* 撚 ("stroke"), *sheng-ssu* 勝似 ("surpass"); adverbs like *cheng* or *cheng-shih* 正是 ("just"), *hun* 渾 ("completely"), *yeh* 也 ("also"), *tu* 都 ("all"), *tsen* or *tsen-sheng* 怎生 ("how"), *ti-ssu* 抵死 ("persistently"); verbal suffixes like *ch'ü* 取 (such as in *liu-ch'ü* 留取, "keep") and *ch'üeh* 卻 (such as in *wang-ch'üeh* 忘卻, "forget"); and adverbial suffixes like *ti* 地 and *te* 得. Such expressions contribute to the informality and liveliness of the style.

When elegant diction is used, imagery is often present. Su Shih uses a great many images of comparison, as well as a considerable number of images of transference and substitution. Generally, his images are natural and effortless rather than elaborate or carefully wrought. Many of them are quite conventional, but sometimes we encounter more striking ones. In addition to the ones we have seen in Nos. 21, 22, and 23, a few more examples may be given. In one lyric presented to a friend who was leaving his post as prefect of Huang-chou, Su writes, "I shall, together with the local people, drink the benevolence you are leaving behind: a whole river of strong wine!"[45] In another lyric, he describes a girl musician with the words, "Her exquisite thoughts are like a fountain, which washes away the idle sorrows of fifteen years."[46] Some images involve double comparisons, or comparison combined with transference. For instance, in one lyric, the waves of the river in spring are first called "snowy" and then compared to a vast expanse of wine swelling up.[47]

Some of Su's images, though conventional, are noteworthy because of their recurrence in various lyrics. Take these lines from different lyrics: "The affairs of this world are like a great dream," "Human life is like a dream," "Past and present are like a dream," "Fifteen years' time is truly like a dream," "Human life is like a sojourning," "Human life is like an inn," "This life is like a posthouse," "Years and months pass like shuttles," "In human life, why so many comings and goings like shuttles?"[48] These images, each common enough in itself, become remarkable through their

---

[45] *Ibid.*, p. 296; Lung Yü-sheng, 2, p. 21.
[46] CST, p. 322.
[47] *Ibid.*, p. 290.
[48] *Ibid.*, pp. 284, 282, 302, 289, 284, 286, 312, 278.

recurrence, for they reveal the poet's preoccupation with the passing of time and his belief in the illusory nature of human life. The use of erudite language is one of Su's original contributions to the development of the lyric. Although some critics consider such language unsuitable for the lyric, this is based on a narrow and conservative conception of the genre. If we take a broader view and conceive of the lyric as a poetic genre with unlimited potential, then there is no reason why one should not write lyrics in an erudite style. The fact that Su has done so, therefore, should be regarded as an extension of the realm of the lyric (stylistically speaking) rather than a deviation from the mainstream of lyric poetry.

The erudite style is perceptible in the use of particles (known in Chinese as *hsü-tzu* or "empty [i.e. functional, non-concrete] words") normally found in Classical Chinese prose, and of allusions and quotations. Before Su, lyricists would rarely use such prose particles as *yi* 矣 (final particle indicating completion of action), *chih* 之 (possessive particle), or *tsai* 哉 (final exclamatory particle) in a lyric, yet he used them repeatedly. When they occur, they introduce a deliberately prosaic effect and a more relaxed rhythm, in contrast to the more heightened langauge and tighter rhythm generally found in the lyrics of his predecessors. Even though some readers may not like this kind of style, it undeniably represents a new advance in the exploration of language.

Su Shih's allusions are remarkable not only because of the frequency of their occurrence (more than two hundred allusions occur in his three hundred and two extant lyrics) but also because of the variety of their sources and their poetic effects. In contrast to previous lyricists, who had confined themselves to general allusions (those to common knowledge and familiar stories), Su used numerous specific allusions to all kinds of writings. These specific allusions fall into four categories. First, allusions to the Confucian classics, such as the *Book of Poetry,* the *Analects,* and the *Mencius.* Second, those to Taoist and Buddhist works. Numerically, these two categories are not very prominent: there are a dozen or so Confucian allusions, a similar number of Taoist ones (most of which are to the *Chuang Tzu*), and five or six Buddhist ones; nonetheless they are highly significant, since Su appears to be the first one to have used them in *lyrics.* The third and largest category consists of historical allusions (more than a hundred), which include not just references to famous historical figures but also allusions to particular passages in historical works. Poetically, they are the most important. The fourth category consists of about thirty allusions to earlier literature. These are sometimes difficult to distinguish from "echoes" or "borrowings" and are less significant than the third category. We cannot draw strict lines of distinction between the different categories, such as between "historical" and "literary" allusions, or between "Taoist" and "literary," but the above classification will give some indication of Su's preferences in the use of allusions.

Apart from generally adding to the learned tone of many of Su's lyrics, allusions can produce certain specific effects. In the first place, they can introduce a wider perspective of time and enable a poem to transcend its immediate context. Allusions of this kind assume a symbolic significance, for the persons and events alluded to become concrete representations of abstract or universal phenomena. For instance, in No. 22 quoted above, Chou Yü is not just a hero but a symbol of heroism, and the battle of the Red Cliff is not just one battle but a symbol of all war. Secondly, an allusion can draw an analogy between the poet himself, or the person to whom the poem is addressed, and some historical or legendary figure. For example, Su Shih alluded many times to the poet-recluse T'ao Ch'ien, with whom he felt a great affinity, so much so that he even claimed (perhaps playfully) to be T'ao's reincarnation.[49] By means of these allusions, he asserted his own moral integrity and otherworldliness. Thirdly, an allusion can be used to achieve a humorous effect. In a lyric addressed to an unidentified friend, Su alludes to *The Gentle Maiden* in the *Book of Poetry:*

> Who has seen the gentle maiden at the tower of
>   the city wall?
> You, sir, sing of the red pipe day and night![50]

[49] *Ibid.,* p. 298.
[50] *Ibid.,* p. 304; see also J. J. Y. Liu, I, pp. 22–23, 105–06.

Since the original poem describes a lover waiting anxiously for the "gentle maiden" at the tower of the city wall while looking at the "red pipe," a gift from her, the allusion pokes gentle fun at the poet's friend for his lovesickness.

Su did not use quotations very often, but to have used them at all in lyrics was another new departure in the use of language. Since quotations are in fact extended allusions, they naturally have similar effects. For example, in a lyric presented to a friend, Su quotes, in abbreviated form, Confucius's remark about Prime Minister Tzu-wen: "Three times he served as Prime Minister without showing joy, and three times he relinquished his post without showing displeasure."[51]   Obviously, the quotation draws an analogy between the poet's friend and the worthy minister praised by Confucius.   Or when Su quotes several times T'ao Ch'ien's famous line, "O, let me return,"[52] he is not only expressing his wish to go home but also comparing himself to the earlier poet.   Apart from such specific effects, quotations from familiar classics, when they occur in lyrics, make the reader feel the pleasure of recognition combined with surprise, like meeting an old friend in an unexpected place.

Some of Su's lyrics consist entirely of quotations from earlier poets,[53] the results of the practice known as *chi-chü* or "collecting lines." They are clever pastiche rather than serious poetry, and they demonstrate the "collector's" erudition, memory, and ingenuity rather than creative talent.

A somewhat different case is presented by what is called *yin-k'uo* or "beveling," which refers to taking an existing poem or piece of prose and rewriting the words to suit a given lyric meter. The results, as I suggested in the introduction, may be simply called "adaptations." Su made several adaptations of the works of T'ao Ch'ien, Han Yü, and others.[54] Such adaptations are comparable to new arrangements of existing music, and involve some technical dexterity.

[51] CST, p. 312.
[52] *Ibid.*, pp. 278, 307, 312, 325.
[53] *Ibid.*, p. 292.
[54] *Ibid.*, pp. 280 (Han Yü), 289 (Tu Mu), 307 (T'ao Ch'ien), 308 (Emperor Wu of Han), 314 (Chang Chih-ho).

Yet another sign of Su's verbal wit and technical virtuosity is seen in a number of palindromic lyrics, in each of which every line read backwards forms the next line.[55] Of course, he was enabled to do so by the highly flexible nature of Chinese syntax, but his superiority over other players of this literary game lies in the apparent naturalness of these lyrics.

As we have noted before, Su sometimes disregarded prosodic rules. However, this does not mean that he was indifferent to prosody, only that he exercised greater freedom than others. For example, his uses of the initial monosyllabic segment and of enjambment are frequent and varied. The former occurs more than fifty times, and the latter about two hundred and fifty. His interest in prosodic experiments can be further witnessed by the fact that over twenty new meters or new variant forms of existing meters originated with him. Altogether eighty-four meters (including variant forms) are used in his lyrics, of which forty-seven are "little airs" and thirty-seven "slow lyrics." The shortest consists of twenty-five syllables, the longest of two hundred and fourteen.[56]

Nor is it true, as some of his detractors claimed, that he was ignorant of music, since we know that he wrote words for zither (*ch'in*) and lute (*p'i-pa*) music[57] and sang his own lyrics.[58] It would be nearer the mark to say that he regarded music as secondary in importance to poetic qualities, and freed the lyric from its dependency on music. We may therefore call him the originator of the "literati lyric" (*wen-jen tz'u*).

---

[55] *Ibid.*, pp. 304–05.
[56] The shortest is *Yü-fu*, the longest *Ch'i-shih*.
[57] CST, pp. 280 (preface), 331 (preface).
[58] Hu Yün-yi, pp. 10–11.

CHAPTER 4

Subtlety and Sophistication

Chou Pang-yen (1056-1121)[1]

Whereas Su Shih freed the lyric from its dependency on music, Chou Pang-yen, who was Superintendent of the Bureau of Grand Music, reunited the two; and whereas the former emphasized intellectuality, the latter confined himself mainly to the exploration of personal emotions, especially love. Yet it would not be true to say that Chou was a literary reactionary who simply reverted to an earlier tradition, for in his hands the lyric reached new heights of subtlety and sophistication both in its modes of sensibility and in its modes of expression. His lyrics are distinguished by the complexity of their poetic worlds and the intricacy of their verbal structures.

No. 25.

桃溪不作從容住
秋藕絕來無續處
當時相候赤欄橋
今日獨尋黃葉路

---

[1] For Chou Pang-yen's life, see Wang Kuo-wei, II. Wang gave Chou's date of birth as 1051, but according to Lu K'an-ju and Feng Yüan-chün (p. 645), it should be 1056.

烟中列岫青無數
雁背夕陽紅欲暮
人如風後入江雲
情似雨餘黏地絮

Yü-lou Ch'un

t'ao   hsi   pu   tso   ts'ung-jung chu   (dʼiu)
peach   stream   not   make   leisurely   stay

ch'iu   ou   chüeh-lai   wu   hsü   ch'u   (tsʼiwo)
autumn   lotus-root   sever-since   no   join   place

tang-shih   hsiang   hou   ch'ih   lan   ch'iao
that-time   (prefix)   wait   red   banister   bridge

chin-jih   tu   hsün   huang   yeh   lu   (luo)
to-day   alone   seek   yellow   leaf   road

yen   chung   lieh   hsiu   ch'ing   wu   shu   (șiu)
mist   amid   arrange   peak   green   no   number

yen   pei   hsi-yang   hung   yü   mu   (muo)
wild-goose   back   setting-sun   red   about-to   evening

jen   ju   feng   hou   ju   chiang   yün
man   like   wind   after   enter   river   cloud

ch'ing   ssu   yü   yü   nien   ti   hsü   (siwo)²
love   like   rain   left-over   stick   ground   catkin

No leisurely stay by the Peach-blossom Stream—
The autumn lotus-root, once severed, cannot be re-joined.
Then: waiting for her on the red-banistered bridge;
Now: alone seeking the road covered with yellow leaves.

²CST, p. 617. For variant readings see Yang Yi-lin, 10, pp. 5b–6a.

In the mist, numberless green peaks stand in a row;
On the wild goose's back, the setting sun reddens before dusk.
A wind-blown cloud entering the river: that's me;
Willow catkins clinging to the ground after rain: that's love.

Note

St. 1, l. 1. Peach-blossom Stream. This alludes to the story about Liu Ch'en and Juan Chao, who met two immortal ladies and lived with them. In the original story, the location is T'ien-t'ai Mountain, but many writers confuse it with the Peach-blossom Fountain, the utopian land described in T'ao Ch'ien's famous allegory. Here the allusion signifies a romantic love affair.

St. 1, l. 2. There is a common expression, *ou tuan ssu lien,* "the lotus-root is broken but the silk-like filament remains connected," an expression that originated from a poem by Meng Chiao (751–814) and is used to describe a person's inability to forget a past love.[3] Further, *ou* 藕 ("lotus-root") puns on *ou* 偶 ("mate"), and *ssu* 絲 ("silk" or "filament"), as I pointed out once before, puns on *ssu* 思 ("thought" or "longing").[4]

Meter[5]

```
干 - 干 + / - - + a
± + 干 - / - + + a
+ - 干 + / + - - o
± + 干 - / - + + a

干 - 干 + / - - + a
干 + 干 - / - + + a
干 - 干 + / + - - o
± + ± - / - + + a
```

Commentary

A series of multiple contrasts, upon which the structure of the whole lyric is built, drive home the main theme—the contrast be-

---

[3]Meng Chiao, 3, p. 1b, Cf. J. J. Y. Liu, II, p. 128.
[4]See above, p. 36.
[5]Cf. TL, 7, p. 7a; TP, 12, pp. 10 a–b; TF, 3, p. 46a; Yang Yi-lin, 8, p. 17a.

tween past happy love and present loneliness. We may first observe the contrast in color between the red peach-blossoms and
the pale lotus-root, and that between the red banisters and the
yellow leaves. The two red objects are associated with spring,
youth, and joy (in China, red is a lucky color and is used for
weddings, birthdays, and New Year celebrations), while the pallid
and yellow colors signify autumn, decay, and desolation. Moreover, it is possible, as Yü P'ing-po ingeniously suggested, that the
"red-banistered bridge" is associated, through earlier poetic contexts, with the willow tree in spring.[6] If so, then there is a further
underlying contrast between the fresh green willows of spring and
the fallen yellow leaves of autumn. The color contrast continues
in the second stanza, but with somewhat different roles for red
and green to play: the green peaks represent the unchanging
aspects of Nature, whereas the red setting sun symbolizes the
passing of time. Simultaneous with these color contrasts are a
series of contrasts between static and kinetic images. The first
line implies a wanderer always on the move and unable to stay
even in a paradise of love, in contrast to the lotus-root (line 2)
that, once severed, remains the same. In the next couplet, the
image of the motionless waiting lover contrasts with the traveler
walking and seeking his way. Likewise, in the second stanza, the
immobile peaks contrast with the flying wild goose, and the wind-
blown cloud contrasts with the catkins stuck on the ground.
These contrasting images emphasize, on the one hand, the
speaker's rootless existence, and, on the other hand, the enduring
nature of love.

The language of this lyric is elegant but neither artificial nor
pedantic. Apart from the well-known allusion in the opening line,
there are no specific allusions, although, as previous commentators
have pointed out, there are many expressions derived, consciously
or unconsciously, from earlier poets.[7] These derived expressions
are so skillfully blended together that they seem perfectly natural

---

[6] Yü P'ing-po, pp. 9–20.

[7] Ch'en Yüan-lung, 10, p. 3a; Yü P'ing-po, *loc.cit.* Line 2 in the second
stanza may also echo Wei Chuang's line, "The wild goose carries the slanting sun into the city of Wei" (Wei Chuang, p. 99).

and homogeneous. Moreover, sometimes Chou Pang-yen endows a borrowed expression with a totally new significance. For example, the image of the willow catkin stuck on the ground in the final line is derived from a line by the Buddhist monk Tao-ch'ien (styled Ts'an-liao-tzu, a friend of Su Shih's): "My meditating mind (*ch'an-hsin*) has already become the willow catkin clinging to the mud."[8] But whereas in the original line the image symbolizes a Ch'an master's mind that can no longer be moved by earthly passions, in the present lyric it is used to represent the opposite state of mind—that of persistent love.

No. 26

瑞龍吟

章台路
還見褪粉梅梢
試花桃樹
愔愔坊曲人家
定巢燕子
歸來舊處

黯凝佇
因念箇人癡小
乍窺門戶
侵晨淺約宮黃
障風映袖
盈盈笑語

[8]Ch'en Yüan-lung, *loc.cit.*

前度劉郎重到
訪鄰尋里
同時歌舞
惟有舊家秋娘
聲價如故
吟牋賦筆
猶記燕台句
知誰伴名園露飲
東城閒步
事與孤鴻去

探春盡是傷離意緒
官柳低金縷
歸騎晚
纖纖池塘飛雨
斷腸院落
一簾風絮

Jui-lung Yin

	Chang-t'ai		*lu*	*(luo)*	
	Chang-terrace		road		

huan	*chien*	*t'ui*	*fen*	*mei*	*shao*
again	see	shed	powder	plum	twig

shih	*hua*	*t'ao*	*shu*	*(z̠iu)*
try	flower	peach	tree	

yin-yin	*fang-ch'ü*	*jen*	*chia*
quiet-quiet	pleasure-quarter	people	house

ting   ch'ao   yen-tzu
settle   nest   swallow

kuei-lai   chiu   ch'u   (tś'iwo)
return   old   place

    an   ning   chu   (â'iwo)
    sadly   freeze   stand

yin   nien   ke-jen   ch'ih   hsiao
therefore   recall   this-person   silly   young

cha   k'uei   men-hu   (γuo)
first   peep   door

ch'in-ch'en   ch'ien   yüeh   kung   huang
early-morning   lightly   paint   palace   yellow

chang   feng   ying   hsiu
screen   wind   shine   sleeve

ying-ying   hsiao   yü   (ngiu)
lissome   laugh   talk

ch'ien-tu   Liu   lang   ch'ung   tao
former-time   Liu   young-man   again   arrive

fang   lin   hsün   li
visit   neighbor   seek   lane

t'ung-shih   ke   wu   (miu)
same-time   sing   dance

wei   yu   chiu   chia   Ch'iu-niang
only   be   old   house   Autumn-mistress

sheng   chia   ju   ku   (kuo)
fame   price   like   before

yin   chien   fu   pi
chant   paper   compose   brush

yu   chi   Yen-t'ai   chü   (kiu)
still   remember   Yen-terrace   lines

chih   shui   pan   ming   yüan   lu   yin
know   who   accompany   famous   garden   uncovered   drink

   tung   ch'eng   hsien   pu   (b'uo)
   east   city   leisurely   pace

   shih   yü   ku   hung   ch'ü   (k'iwo)
   event   with   lonely   wild-goose   go

t'an   ch'un   chin   shih   shang   li   yi-hsü   (ziwo)
search   spring   all   be   lament   separation   feeling

   kuan   liu   ti   chin   lü   (liu)
   official   willow   lower   gold   thread

     kuei   chi   wan
     return   ride   late

   hsien-hsien   ch'ih-t'ang   fei   yü   (jiu)
   fine-fine   pond   fly   rain

     tuan-ch'ang   yüan-lo
     break-heart   courtyard

yi   lien   feng   hsü   (siwo)[9]
one   curtain   wind   willow-catkin

By the Chang-t'ai road,
Once more I see the plum twigs shed their powder,
The peach-trees try out their flowers.
In a quiet, quiet house in the pleasure quarters,
The swallows settling down in their nests
Have returned to their old homes.

Sadly I stand transfixed,
Remembering her—a naïve young girl,
Peeping at the door for the first time,
Her eyebrows lightly painted with yellow in courtly fashion at
dawn,

[9]CST, p. 595. For variant readings see Yang Yi-lin, 1, pp. 1a–b. For
line 4, I have adopted the reading *fang-ch'ü* 坊 曲 instead of *fang-mo*
坊 陌, since the former refers to the pleasure quarters. Cf. note on line 4,
and Yang Shen, 2, p. 10b.

A brilliant sleeve screening her from the wind—
So lissome was she, laughing and talking.

The "young Master Liu" of those days has come again,
Enquiring the neighbors, seeking the street:
Of all her singing and dancing companions
Only Mistress Autumn of the old house
Is still as popular as before.
The writing paper and poetic brush
Still remember the "Terrace of Yen" poems,
But with whom is she now drinking casually in a famous garden,
Or taking a leisurely walk in the eastern city?
Everything is gone with the lonely wild goose!
Searching for Spring, I find nothing but the grief of separation.
The wayside willows lower their golden threads.
At nightfall I ride home,
As a flying drizzle falls over the ponds.
In the heart-breaking courtyard
Wind-blown willow catkins fill the curtain.

Notes

St. 1, l. 1. Chang-t'ai road. See note on No. 8, st. 1, l. 5.
l. 4. Pleasure quarters. As the Ming poet and critic Yang Shen
(1488-1559) pointed out, the expression *fang-ch'ü* in T'ang times
referred to the words of Ch'ang-an, where the houses of courtesans
were located, and Chou Pang-yen probably used it in the same
sense.
St. 2, l. 4. Eyebrows painted with yellow. The fashion for
court ladies to paint their eyebrows with yellow is referred to in
various earlier poems.[10]
St. 3, l. 1. The whole line is derived from a poem by Liu Yü-hsi
(772-842). Liu first wrote a poem on the peach-blossoms at the
Hsüan-tu Taoist Temple in 815. After fourteen years, when he
revisited the place, he found that all the peach-trees had disappeared, and thereupon wrote another poem, which contains the
lines, "Where has the Taoist who planted the peach-trees gone?

[10] Yang Shen, 2, pp. 2a–b.

The young Master Liu of those days has come again!"[11] At the same time, the line also alludes to Liu Ch'en. (See note on No. 25, line 1).

l. 4. Mistress Autumn. Ch'iu-niang; at least two famous T'ang courtesans had this name, so it seems better to take it as a general substitute for a courtesan than as a specific allusion.[12]

l. 7. "Terrace of Yen." A group of love poems by Li Shang-yin, who thereby won the admiration of a young girl named Willow Branch. See Liu, *The Poetry of Li Shang-yin,* pp. 68–77, 138–43.

l. 8. Drinking casually. *Lu-yin,* literally "drinking with one's head uncovered." The phrase was used to describe the poet Shih Yen-nien (994–1041).[13]

l. 9. Eastern City. This alludes to a poem by Tu Mu (803–852) about a girl named Chang Hao-hao. According to the poem and its preface, Tu first met her when she was thirteen and just beginning her career as a singing girl. Three years later, she became an official's concubine. After another two years, he saw her again in the *eastern city* of Lo-yang, where she had become a serving maid in a tavern.[14]

l. 12. Wayside willows. Literally "official willows," i.e., willows planted by the government.

Meter[15]

```
        ∓  -  +  a
  -  +  /  +  +  -  -  o
     +  -  ∓  +  a
  -  -  /  ∓  +  /  ∓  -  o
     ±  -  +  +  o
     -  -  +  +  a
```

[11]Liu Yü-hsi, 24, pp. 3a–b, quoted in T'ang Kuei-chang, IV, p. 87; Yü P'ing-po, *loc.cit.*

[12]See Cheng Ch'ien, I, p. 62.

[13]Ch'en Yüan-lung, *loc. cit.*

[14]Feng Chi-wu, 1, pp. 14b–15a.

[15]Cf. TL, 37, pp. 13b–14b; TP, 20, p. 8b; TF, 7, *shang,* pp. 85a–b. These, and the diagram given in the present book, mark only the Level and Oblique Tones. For finer distinctions among the Oblique Tones, see Yang Yi-lin, 1, p. 1a.

```
                    +  -  +  a
        干  +  /  +  -  -  +  o
            +  -  干  +  a
    -  -  /  ±  +  /  -  -  o
        干  -  ±  +  o
        -  -  +  +  a

      -  +  /  -  -  /  -  +  o
        +  -  干  +  o
        干  -  -  +  a
    干  +  /  +  -  /  -  -  o
        -  +  -  +  a
        -  -  ±  +  o
    干  +  /  -  -  +  a
  -  -  +  /  -  -  ±  +  o
        -  -  干  +  a
    +  +  /  -  -  +  a
  +  -  +  +  /  -  -  +  +  a
    干  +  /  -  -  +  a
        -  +  +  o
  -  -  /  干  -  /  -  +  a
    干  -  +  +  o
    ±  -  干  +  a
```

Commentary

The speaker's recollection of a young courtesan and his present sadness are revealed in an oblique manner, mainly through literary allusions. Apart from the allusions mentioned above, the whole lyric (as Chou Chi pointed out)[16] is a variation on the well-known poem by Ts'ui Hu (*fl.* 796): "Last year, on this day, inside this door,/ Her face and the peach-blossoms reflected each other's redness./ Where is her face now?/ The peach-blossoms still smile in the spring wind."[17]   And Ts'ui's poem is said to have come into being this way.[18]   As a young man, Ts'ui once wandered alone outside the city and came upon a quiet and isolated house. After

16Chou Chi, I, p. 7, "eyebrow comment."
17CTS, 368 (p. 4,148).
18Meng Ch'i, pp. 5a–b.

he had knocked on the door for a long time, a young girl *peeped at the door* and asked him who he was. He told her and asked for a drink, whereupon she gave him some water. Leaning against a *peach-tree*, she looked at him affectionately, but when he made advances to her, she did not respond. Eventually he left. A year later to the day, he went there again, but found the door locked, whereupon he wrote the poem.

In the present lyric, the poet reveals the underlying situation through the various allusions, so that there is no need for him to describe it explicitly, and he is free to concentrate on the expression of the emotions engendered by the situation. In the first stanza, the opening line announces the theme by using the familiar allusion to Chang-t'ai as a euphemism for the gay quarters of the capital. This is further confirmed by the expression *fang-ch'ü* in line 4. At the same time, the mention of peach-trees, while serving the purposes of describing the actual scene and indicating the season, also arouses associations with Liu Ch'en and Ts'ui Hu, thereby hinting at a romantic love story. The swallows returning to their old nests contrast with the speaker, who wishes to return to the girl's home but cannot.

The second stanza is devoted to the speaker's recollection of the girl as she was when he first met her. The phraseology is strongly reminiscent of both the story about Ts'ui Hu and Li Shang-yin's preface to the group of poems he wrote about the girl Willow Branch,[19] so that we get a composite portrait of the heroine of the present lyric and those two other girls. The effect is to make us feel that she is not just one beautiful young girl but the very embodiment of youthful beauty and charm.

The third and longest stanza elaborates on the speaker's present sadness, his futile efforts to find her, his jealousy of her new patron (the allusions to Tu Mu's poem about Chang Hao-hao and to Li Shang-yin's "Terrace of Yen" and "Willow Branch" poems

---

[19] Feng Hao, 5, pp. 37a–b; J. J. Y. Liu, II, pp. 138–39. The preface quoted by Ch'en Yüan-lung differs in places from that in extant editions of Li Shang-yin. He also quotes two lines from a poem addressed to Liu-chih that are not found in any extant edition of Li's works. T'ang Kuei-chang, IV, p. 87, gives these lines as Li's, apparently without having checked existing editions.

all suggest that she is now someone else's concubine), and his loneliness. In the concluding lines, the image of the willows with their drooping branches like golden threads completes the spring scene sketched in the first stanza, that of the flying drizzle produces a forlorn atmosphere, and both images are echoed by the final image of the wind-blown willow catkins, which may symbolize constant wandering (referring either to the speaker or the girl or both), or persistent memories of love (compare the similar image in the previous lyric).

Although the language of this lyric is derivative to a great extent, it is coherent and effective, and the various borrowed expressions are given fresh force. For example, the expression "peach-trees try out their flowers" *(shih hua t'ao-shu)* in stanza 1, line 3, is derived from a poem on new peach-blossoms by Chang Chi (768–830?), which contains the lines, "I planted them more than three year ago,/ This summer, for the first time, they are *trying out* their flowers."[20] But the line gains new force here by being used to form an antithesis with "the plum twigs shed their powder" *(t'ui fen mei shao)* of the preceding line. Similarly, the expression "drinking casually in a famous garden" *(ming yüan lu yin,* stanza 3, line 8) forms an antithesis with "taking a leisurely walk in the eastern city" *(tung ch'eng hsien pu)* in the next line, thus giving both expressions a new formal elegance not present in the original texts from which they are derived.

No. 27.

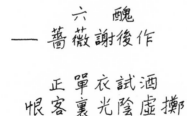

六　醜
—— 薔薇謝後作

正單衣試酒
恨客裏光陰虛擲

---

[20] Yü P'ing-po, p. 43, quoting T'ien Ju-heng of the Ming.

願春暫留
春歸如過翼
一去無迹
為問花何在
夜來風雨
葬楚宮傾國
釵鈿墮處遺香澤
亂點桃蹊
輕翻柳陌
多情為誰追惜
但蜂媒蝶使
時叩窗槅

東園岑寂
漸蒙籠暗碧
靜遶珍叢底
成嘆息
長條故惹行客
似牽衣待話
別情無極
殘英小
強簪巾幘
終不似
一朵釵頭顫裊
向人欹側
漂流處莫趁潮汐
恐斷紅
尚有相思字
何由見得

Liu-ch'ou

—*ch'iang-wei   hsieh   —   hou   tso*
rose   fade   —   after   write

cheng   tan   yi   shih   chiu
just-as   single clothes try   wine

hen   k'e-li   kuang-yin   hsü   chih   (d̂'iäk)
regret visiting light-dark vainly discard

   yüan   ch'un   chan   liu
   wish   spring   temporarily stay

ch'un   kuei   ju   kuo   yi   (iə̂k)
spring   return like   passing wing

   yi   ch'ü   wu   chi   (tsi̯äk)
   once go   no   trace

wei-wen   hua   ho   tsai
ask   flower   where   at

yeh-lai   feng   yü
since-night   wind   rain

tsang   Ch'u   kung   ch'ing-kuo   (kwə̂k)
bury   Ch'u   palace beautiful-woman

ch'ai-t'ien   to   ch'u   yi   hsiang   tse   (d̂'ɒk)
hairpin-filigree   fall   place leave fragrant left-over

   luan   tien   t'ao   hsi
   disorderly   dot   peach   path

   ch'ing   fan   liu   mo   (mɒk)
   lightly   turn   willow road

to-ch'ing   wei   shui   chui-hsi   (si̯äk)
loving-one   for   who   regret-pity

tan   feng   —   mei   tieh   —   shih
only   bee   —   matchmaker   butterfly   —   messenger

   shih   k'ou   ch'uang-ke   (kɛk)
   from-time-to-time knock   window

tung   yüan   ts'en-chi   (dz'iek)
east   garden   quiet

chien   meng-lung   an   pi   (piäk)
gradually thick   dark green

ching   jao   chen   ts'ung   ti
silently circulate precious cluster under

ch'eng   t'an-hsi   (siәk)
become   sigh

ch'ang t'iao ku   je   hsing   k'e   (kᵉk)
long   twig   purposely entangle walking visitor

ssu   ch'ien yi   tai   hua
seem   pull   clothes about-to talk

pieh   ch'ing wu   chi   (g'iәk)
parting   feeling no   limit

ts'an   ying   hsiao
fading   flower small

ch'iang tsan   chin-ts'e   (tsєk)
forcibly pin   turban

chung   pu   ssu
finally not   seem

yi-to   ch'ai-t'ou   ch'an   — niao
one-bloom   hairpin-tip   tremble — waver

hsiang   jen   ch'i-ts'e   (tsiәk)
towards man   lean

p'iao-liu   ch'u   mo   ch'en ch'ao   hsi   (ziäk)
drift-flow   place do-not take   morning-tide evening-tide

k'ung   tuan   hung
fear   broken   red

shang   yu   hsiang-ssu   tzu
still   have   lovesick   word

ho-yu   chien   te   (tәk)[21]
whereby   see   able

---

[21] CST, p. 610. For variant readings see Yang Yi-lin, 7, pp. 18a–b. For the subtitle I have followed Mao Chin's edition. I have not followed CST or Yang Yi-lin for line divisions in all cases.

—Written after the roses have faded

Time for summer clothes and wine-tasting—
How I regret the wasted days and nights away from home!
    I wish Spring would stay for a while,
    But Spring goes back like passing wings,
        Once gone, no trace left.
    If you ask, Where are the flowers?
    Last night, amid wind and rain,
The beautiful ladies of the Ch'u palace were buried.
Where their filigreed ornaments fell, they left
    fragrance behind,
    As they dotted the peach-paths at random,
    And lightly fluttered above the willowy roads.
Who is there so loving as to pity their fall?
Only the matchmaker-bees and messenger-butterflies
    Knock on the window from time to time.

        The eastern garden lies quiet,
        Gradually overgrown with dark green.
    A silent stroll beneath the precious clusters
        Turns into a sigh.
The long twigs purposely entangle the passer-by,
    As if pulling his clothes, about to speak,
        With endless parting sorrow.
        A tiny remaining bloom
    I force myself to wear on the turban,
        But after all it's not like
One that softly wavers at the tip of a hairpin
        And leans towards you.
Ah, do not drift away by the morning or evening tide!
    For I fear that on the fallen red
    There may still be words of lovesickness—
        How could anyone see them then?

Notes

    St. 1, l. 1. Summer clothes. *Tan-yi,* literally "single (i.e., un-
lined) clothes."
    l. 8. The original for "beautiful ladies" is *ch'ing-kuo,* literally
"(those who can) overthrow a country," derived from a song by Li

Yen-nien (second century B.C.) about a beauty who, with one glance, could overthrow a city and, with a second glance, overthrow a country. The mention of Ch'u palace alludes to the story about Court ladies who starved themselves to death to keep slim. (Cf. above, p. 87).

l. 14. Window. Some commentators explain the word *ke* as "lattice," but according to Hsia Ch'eng-t'ao it means the same thing as *ch'uang* or "window."[22]

St. 2, l. 5. The word translated as "entangle" is *je*, which is used in a double sense: the long and prickly twigs of the roses pull the sleeve of the passer-by, thus entangling him physically, and at the same time arouse associations of parting sorrow, thus entangling him emotionally.[23]

ll. 14–15. These lines allude to the story about Lu Wu, who saw a fallen red leaf drifting in the canal that led from the palace, with this poem written on it: "How rapidly does the water flow!/ Deep in the palace, nothing to do all day./ Diligently I ask the red leaf:/ Go forth into the human world!"[24]

Meter[25]

```
        +  /  -  -  +  +  o
  +  +  +  /  -  -  -  +  a
     +  -  +  ∓  o
  -  -  /  -  +  +  a
     +  +  -  +  a
  +  +  /  -  -  +  o
     ±  -  ∓  +  o
     +  /  ±  -  -  +  a
  -  -  +  +  /  -  -  +  a
     +  +  -  -  o
  -  -  ±  +  a
  -  -  /  +  -  /  -  +  a
     +  /  -  -  +  +  o
        ∓  +  -  +  a
```

[22] Hsia Ch'eng-t'ao and Sheng T'ao-ch'ing, p. 92.
[23] *Ibid.*
[24] T'ang Kuei-chang, IV, p. 92; Cheng Ch'ien, I, p. 62; Hu Yün-yi, p. 134.
[25] Cf. TL, 20, pp. 12a–b; TP, 38, pp. 32b–3a; TF, 3, p. 70b; Yang Yi-lin, *loc. cit.*

```
            -   -   ∓   +   a
      +   /   -   -   +   +   a
      +   +   /   -   -   +   o
                -   +   +   a
  ∓   -   /   +   +   /   -   +   a
      +   /   -   -   ±   +   o
          +   -   -   +   a
              -   -   +   o
      ±   -   -   +   a
          -   +   +   o
  +   +   /   -   -   /   +   +   o
      +   -   -   +   a
-   -   +   /   ±   +   -   +   a
          +   +   -   o
      +   +   /   -   -   +   a
          -   -   +   +   a
```

Commentary

This lyric challenges comparison with the one by Su Shih on the willow catkin (No. 23), since both reveal highly imaginative poetic worlds through apparently trivial objects. But whereas Su approaches his subject intellectually and objectively, first puzzling over the nature of the catkin and then endowing it with symbolic significance, Chou starts with an expression of subjective emotions and then finds their "objective correlative" in the faded roses. The poem begins by lamenting the passing of Spring, and, by implication, of the poet's own youth, before turning to bewail the fate of the roses. The comparison of the fallen roses to palace beauties suggests the writer's love for a woman, whose youth and beauty, he fears, may also fade away. The suggestion of a love affair is strengthened by such words as "loving" *(to-ch'ing)*, "matchmaker" *(mei)*, and "messenger" *(shih,* between two lovers), and, in the next stanza, the personification of the rose as a woman reluctant to part from her lover. The separation of the lovers is further hinted at by the contrast between the half-faded rose that now adorns the man's turban, and the recollection of the full-blown rose that once stood at the tip of the woman's hairpin, gently wavering and leaning towards the man, like the woman herself. Finally, by borrowing the allusion to the red leaf that carried a palace lady's message of loneliness and craving for love, the poet expresses similar sentiments, now attached to the fallen red roses. The whole lyric wonderfully integrates the emotional world of regret, homesickness, longing for an absent woman, and loneliness, with the physical world of roses, peach and willow trees, bees and butterflies, and the imaginery world of dying palace beauties with their ornaments and perfumes, so that several planes of reality are presented at the same time, and various kinds of experience (emotional, sensuous, and imaginative) are synthesized.

Stylistically, this lyric is not as allusive as the preceding one, but it is no less elegant. There are a number of original images, namely, the comparisons of Spring to "passing wings" and of bees and butterflies to matchmakers and messengers respectively, and the personification of the rose in the second stanza. In form, the most remarkable ones among these images are "matchmaker-bees" and "messenger-butterflies" (*feng-mei tieh-shih,* literally, "bee-matchmakers" and "butterfly-messengers," but I have inverted the two terms of each compound image to conform to English morphology; Cf. "worker bees" and "carrier-pigeons"). Each of these images brackets together the two objects compared, without using any verb to indicate the comparison, so that greater conciseness and novelty are achieved.

No. 28

滿庭芳
夏日溧水無想山作

風老鶯雛
雨肥梅子
午陰嘉樹清圓
地卑山近
衣潤費鑪烟
人靜烏鳶自樂
小橋外新綠濺濺
憑闌久
黃蘆苦竹
擬泛九江船

年年
如社燕
飄流瀚海
來寄修椽
且莫思身外
長近尊前
顦顇江南倦客
不堪聽急管繁絃
歌筵畔
先安簟枕
容我醉時眠

Man-t'ing Fang

—hsia-jih	Li-shui	Wu-hsiang	Shan	tso
summer-day	Li-shui	No-thought	Hill	write

feng	lao	ying	ch'u
wind	age	oriole	chick

Yü	fei	mei-tzu
rain	fatten	plum-child

wu	yin	chia	shu	ch'ing	yüan	(jiwän)
noon	shade	fine	tree	clear	round	

ti	pei	shan	chin
place	low	hill	near

yi	jun	fei	lu	yen	(·ien)
clothes	damp	cost	censer	smoke	

jen	ching	wu-yüan	tzu	lo
people	quiet	kite	self	enjoy

hsiao	ch'iao	wai	hsin	lu	chien-chien	(tsien)
little	bridge	beyond	new	green	splutter	

p'ing	lan	chiu
lean	railing	long

huang	lu	k'u	chu
yellow	reed	bitter	bamboo

ni	fan	Chiu-chiang	ch'uan	(dź'iwän)
plan	float	Chiu-chiang	boat	

nien	—	nien	(nien)
year	—	year	

ju	she	yen
like	sacrifice	swallow

p'iao-liu	han-hai
drift-flow	great-desert

lai	chi	hsiu	ch'uan	(d̂'iwän)
come	lodge	long	rafter	

> ch'ieh   mo   ssu   shen-wai
> temporarily do-not think body-beyond
>
>   ch'ang chin   tsun   ch'ien   (dz'ien)
>   long   near   wine-jar front
>
> ch'iao-ts'ui Chiang-nan   chüan k'e
> haggard   River-south tired traveller
>
> pu   k'an   t'ing chi   kuan fan   hsien   (yien)
> not bear   hear   fast pipe numerous string
>
>   ko   yen   p'an
>   song feast beside
>
>   hsien an   tien   chen
>   first settle mattress pillow
>
>   jung   wo   tsui   shih mien   (mien)²⁶
>   allow me   drunk time sleep

—Written on a summer's day at Thought-free
  Hill in Li-shui

     The wind has aged young orioles,
     The rain fattened baby plums,
  The noontide shades of fine trees are clear and round.
     On these lowlands near the hill,
  Clothes are damp and need to be dried with incense smoke.
  People being quiet, the kites enjoy themselves.
Beyond the little bridge, the fresh green water splutters on.
     Leaning on the rails for a long time,
     Amid yellow reeds and bitter bamboos,
  I wish to sail down to Chiu-chiang.

          Year after year,
       Like the seasonal swallow
     Drifting over the great desert
  And coming to lodge on the long rafters!

²⁶CST, pp. 601–2; Yang Yi-lin, 4, p. 1a. The sub-title is added from Mao
Chin.

last three words of Tu Fu's line, *hung chan yü fei mei*[31] ("Red bursts: rain fattens plums"), added the suffix *tzu*, and matched the whole line against *feng lao ying ch'u* ("Wind ages oriole chicks"), which is apparently his own creation. The result is the antithetical couplet at the beginning of the lyric. Line 3 is adapted from Liu Yü-hsi's *jih wu shu yin cheng*[32] ("At midday, trees' shades are direct"), but by substituting *ch'ing yüan* ("clear and round") for *cheng* ("direct"), Chou adds vividness to the description. Line 6, according to Ch'en Yüan-lung,[33] is taken from Tu Fu with the addition of the word *tzu* ("by themselves"), although the line does not appear in any extant edition of Tu. Assuming that Ch'en knew a poem by Tu Fu now lost to us, we may regard this as another example of borrowing, with the added word suggesting the contrast between the birds' enjoying themselves and the speaker's unhappiness. In stanza 2, lines 5–6 are again borrowed from Tu Fu. As quoted by Ch'en Yüan-lung,[34] Tu's original lines read:

莫思身外無窮事
且盡尊前有限杯

mo	*ssu*	*shen*	*wai*	*wu-ch'iung*	*shih*
do-not	think	person	beyond	no-end	thing

ch'ieh	*chin*	*tsun*	*ch'ien*	*yu-hsien*	*pei*
temporarily	finish	wine-jar	front	limited	cup

but in extant editions of Tu Fu, the second line is a little different:

ch'ieh	*chin*	*sheng-ch'ien*	*yu-hsien*	*pei*[35]
temporarily	finish	alive-time	limited	cup

If the version Chou knew was the same as that quoted by Ch'en, what he did was simply abbreviate Tu's lines. If, on the other

[31] Tu Fu, p. 283, quoted by Ch'en Yüan-lung and others.
[32] Liu Yü-hsi, 22, p. 5a; quoted by Ch'en Yüan-lung and others.
[33] Ch'en Yüan-lung, *loc.cit.*
[34] *Ibid.*
[35] Tu Fu, p. 359.

hand, the version he knew was the same as the extant one, then he changed the expression *sheng-ch'ien* ("while still alive"), to *tsun ch'ien* ("before the wine jar") to make the meaning clear, since the word for "winecup" *(pei)* had been omitted. Finally, the last line of the poem echoes T'ao Ch'ien's famous remark to a friend: "I'm drunk and want to sleep, you may go!"[36] All these borrowings and echoes not only serve the purpose of describing the present situation and the poet's feelings, but also suggest that he wishes to emulate the earlier poets in their philosophic outlook on life, and perhaps in their poetic achievements as well.

Chou Pang-yen has been hailed by many traditional Chinese critics as the supreme master of the lyric, the great synthesizer of all previous styles, the perfect model for all later lyricists, and the patriarch of the orthodox school.[37] He has also been condemned by some modern critics for his alleged "formalism" and "emptiness of content."[38] Both these views are biased. It is true that he synthesized certain styles, especially those of Liu Yung and Ch'in Kuan, but his lyrics show little influence of Su Shih, either in theme or in style. Technically, he is perhaps the most accomplished craftsman among lyricists with regard to the finer points of versification, and apparently his lyrics were perfectly suited to the music for which they were intended, but from a purely literary point of view he cannot be called the greatest poet in the lyric genre. As for "formalism," this label can be applied with more justification to Chou's imitators than to himself, for even the few examples given above are enough to convince one that he is concerned not only with formal beauty but with the exploration of emotional experiences. In this he resembles most of the other lyricists discussed in this book (Yen Shu, Ou-yang Hsiu, Liu Yung, and Ch'in Kuan), but he differs from them in that he seems to take a more detached attitude towards emotion. His lyrics generally do not present raw emotion but "emotion recollected in tranquility," although, on the other hand, he does not attain to

[36]Ch'en Yüan-lung, *loc.cit.*, quoting from T'ao's biography.
[37]Chou Chi, I, p. 2, II, p. 2a; Ch'en T'ing-cho, 1, p. 6b; Chiang Chao-lan, p. 3a; all quoted in Chiang Shang-hsien, II, pp. 71–78.
[38]Liu Ta-chieh, *chung*, p. 256; Hu Yün-yi, Foreword, p. 12.

Su Shih's philosophic transcendance of emotion either. With engaging helplessness, he accepts emotion as an inevitable human weakness. In his response to Nature, he is like Yen, Ou-yang, and Ch'in, for he too is attracted by the gentle rather than august aspects of Nature, and he too tends to look at Nature through human emotions. However, his observation is more minute, his imagination capable of greater flights, and his power of empathy more profound, as can be seen from such poems as Nos. 27 and 28.

In his exploration of language as a poetic medium in the lyric genre, Chou is notable for his ability to write in a predominantly elegant style, while freely using colloquialisms without being vulgar on the one hand, and frequently resorting to allusions and derivations without becoming bookish on the other. Certain remarkable prosodic and structural features constitute further contributions he made to the development of poetic language.

The elegance of Chou's language owes not a little to his use of imagery, drawn mostly from the familiar aspects of Nature. In addition to numerous images of comparison, there are unusually large numbers of images of transference (many of which involve personification) and of substitution. In all these types of imagery, the natural world and the human world are constantly intermingled: human beings, attributes, and emotions are often described in terms of natural objects and phenomena, and natural objects and events are sometimes described in human terms. Among images of comparison, the following are of special interest. In one lyric, a budding lotus flower is compared to a pretty girl, whereas in another one a girl's white wrists are compared to "snowy lotus-roots in crystalline fountain water."[39] Similarly, in one context raindrops leaping on fresh lotus flowers are compared to tears, but in another context tears are said to have all turned into autumn night rain.[40] We may also notice some images that describe emotional experiences in terms of sensuous ones: "sorrow as strong as wine," "love as strong as wine," and "the exile's feelings are like intoxication."[41]

[39] CST, p. 602.
[40] Ibid., pp. 603, 606.
[41] Ibid., pp. 597, 623, 627.

Images of transference that do not involve personification include: "Spring has just turned *soft (juan)* 軟 ," "Grievances *pile up (tui-chi)* 堆積," and "Grievances *fill (man)* 滿 a thousand *li* of grass."[42] In these images, the poet transfers attributes and actions from unidentified objects to the things described, to which these attributes and actions are not literally applicable. In some cases, attributes or actions so transferred may be considered human, though it is hardly necessary to take them this way. For example, in the lines "Fragrant grass *carries* mist *in the bosom (huai)* 懷; Thick clouds *hold* rain *in the mouth (hsien)* 街 "; "The setting sun *locks (so)* 鎖 deeply the green-moss-grown gate"; "The window *locks up (so)* elaborate shadows"; "Half an acre of blossoming *wu-t'ung* trees quietly *locks up (so)* a courtyardful of sad rain"; and "The wind *combs (shu)* 梳 ten thousand strands of willow twigs before the pavilion";[43] the effect will hardly be heightened if we try to imagine these actions as being performed by human agents. In some other instances, however, the element of personification is much stronger; "The wind and rain that are *jealous (tu)* 妒 of the flowers"; "The willows *weep (ch'i)* 泣 and the flowers *cry (t'i)* 啼 "; "The dark leaves *cry (t'i)* amid wind and rain"; and "The frosty moon flies here to *accompany (pan)* 伴 the solitary traveller."[44] Many more examples can be found in Chou's lyrics, and we may conclude that he is even more fond of personification than Ch'in Kuan.

Chou's images of substitution are less remarkable than those of transference. A few of the more striking ones are: "Snowy waves turn in the air; powdered skirts whiten the night," where both images are substitutes for pear blossoms; "emerald canopies" and "cold jades" for bamboos; and "iridescent cream and built-up jades" for plum blossoms.[45] Conventional and rather hackneyed images of substitution include "silver hook" for the new moon,

42 *Ibid.*, pp. 608, 617, 611.
43 *Ibid.*, pp. 600, 616, 610, 595, 600.
44 *Ibid.*, pp. 610, 599, 603, 606.
45 *Ibid.*, pp. 610, 603, 601, 609.

"ice wheel" for the full moon, and "delicate phoenix" for a woman.[46]

In addition to images of substitution, Chou also uses metonymy, such as "bronze" for mirror, "black gauze" for an official hat,[47] and the like.

In general, imagery in Chou's lyrics enhances their refinement of style, but at the same time it also tends to render their mode of expression more oblique and correspondingly reduce their immediacy of appeal. That is why the critic Wang Kuo-wei regretted Chou's use of "substitute words."[48] To Wang, the highest kind of poetry has a quality of immediacy or transparency, which he calls *"pu ke,"* literally "not separated" or "not veiled" (from the reader), whereas inferior poetry is *"ke,"* which may be rendered "veiled" or "opaque."[49] Whether or not we accept this as a criterion for the best poetry, it is true that some of Chou's lyrics lack transparency and have an opaque quality, which is due at least in part to images of substitution and similar poetic devices.

Although, as we have noted, Chou's lyrics are predominantly elegant in style, colloquialisms do appear quite often. Sometimes they are mixed with more refined diction, and at other times they form the prevailing tone of a whole lyric. A few examples may be given here: the colloquial pronouns *ni* 你 ("you," twice), *t'a* 他 ("he" or "she," eight times), and *yi* 伊 ("he" or "she," ten times); the verbs *ch'an-ch'ou* 僝僽 ("worry" or "grieve," twice), *p'in* 拚 ("let oneself go"); the adverbs *cheng* 爭 ("how," six times), *hun* 渾 ("wholly"), *sheng* 生 (emphatic); the suffix *erh* 兒 ; the final exclamatory particle *o* 呵 . Such colloquialisms add a lively touch to the style and help prevent it from becoming too artificial.

On the other hand, although he uses many allusions and derivations, these do not render his language pedantic, because of their nature and sources. We encounter about forty general allusions

---

[46]*Ibid.,* pp. 604, 622, 606.

[47]*Ibid.,* pp. 611, 596.

[48]Wang Kuo-wei, I, *shang,* p. 4a. Cf. T'u Ching-i, p. 22.

[49]*Ibid.,* p. 5a. Cf. T'u Ching-i, pp. 27–29. For further discussion, see Hsü Fu-kuan, pp. 118–39.

(those to well-known personages, places, or stories) that are easily recognizable and function as substitutes for common nouns with added associations, and about the same number of specific allusions to earlier literature. In contrast to Su Shih, who, as we have seen, alludes to the Confucian Classics, Taoist and Buddhist writings, historical works, as well as to earlier literature, Chou generally alludes to imaginative literature, occasionally to historical works, only two or three times to legends of Taoist origin (and these are well known and not particularly philosophical in nature), and never to the Confucian Classics. Consequently his allusions contribute to the "literariness" of his style but do not create an impression of bookishness. His derivations too are mostly from earlier imaginative literature and have an effect similar to that of his allusions.

Another reason why Chou's language does not appear bookish is that, again in contrast to Su Shih, he hardly uses any particles commonly used in Classical Chinese prose. However, the presence of allusions and derivations, together with that of images of substitution, further reduces the immediacy of appeal of his lyrics.

Chou's prosody has been studied in considerable detail by such scholars as Hsia Ch'eng-t'ao[50] and Yang Yi-lin.[51] Here I shall merely mention a few important features, based partly on the works of these scholars and partly on my own scrutiny of Chou's lyrics. To begin with, not only does he distinguish Level Tones from Oblique Tones, but he also carefully distinguishes the three kinds of Oblique Tones (Rising, Falling, and Entering). To be sure, he was not the first one to do so, for Yen Shu and Liu Yung had already paid some attention to the use of different kinds of Oblique Tones, as Hsia has shown,[52] but Chou was the first to have consistently observed distinctions among all four tones. Moreover, the tonal distinctions are not made purely for musical effect, but are correlated to the meaning of the words. Special attention is given to the tonal patterns of syllables occupying key positions in a meter and embodying particularly striking words.[53]

[50] Hsia Ch'eng-t'ao, I, pp. 66–76.
[51] Yang Yi-lin, *passim.*
[52] Hsia Ch'eng-t'ao, I, pp. 56–66.
[53] *Ibid.*, p. 69.

With regard to prosodic features that affect both syntax and rhythm, Chou uses enjambment about as often as Su Shih and Ch'in Kuan, though not quite as often as Liu Yung. His uses of the initial monosyllabic segment are more varied than Su's or Ch'in's, and follow a more consistent pattern than Liu's. In general, he uses it as part of a single line or to introduce several lines of unequal length oftener than to precede an antithetical conplet. Patterns that occur most frequently are the following.

1 : 4

漸雨淒風迅

e.g.

chien/	yü	ch'i	feng	hsün[54]
gradually	rain	chilly	wind	fast

1 : 2 : 3

任撲面桃花雨

e.g.

jen/	p'u	mien/	t'ao-hua		yü[55]
let/	dab	face/	peach-blossom		rain

1 : 2 : 4

奈猶被思牽情繞

e.g.

nai/	yu	pei/	ssu	ch'ien	.ch'ing	jao[56]
what-do/	still	by/	longing	entangle	love	surround

1 : 4 : 3

正拂面垂楊堪覽結

e.g.

cheng/	fu	mien	ch'ui	yang	/k'an	lan
just-as/	sweep	face	drooping	willow	/can	gather
						chieh[57]
						knit

[54]CST, p. 606.   [55]Ibid., p. 601.   [56]Ibid., p. 606.   [57]Ibid., p. 598.

1 : 4 : 6

但明河影下還看稀星數點

e.g.

tan	/ming	ho	ying	hsia	/huan k'an	hsi
only	/bright	river	shadow	under	/still look	scarce

			hsing	shu	tien[58]
			star	several	dot

(The "bright river" refers to the Milky Way.)

One particularly interesting structural feature that occurs in several of Chou's lyrics is antithesis in alternate lines instead of consecutive lines. Here is an example:

欲説又休
慮乖芳信
未歌先咽
愁近清觴

yü	shuo	yu	hsiu
about-to	speak	again	stop

lü	kuai	fang	hsin
worry	miss	fragrant	news

wei	ko	hsien	yeh
not-yet	sing	first	choke

ch'ou	chin	ch'ing	shang[59]
grieve	near	clear	wine-cup

The first and third lines quoted form an antithesis, and so do the second and fourth lines. Again, Chou was not the first one to use this device, but the first to develop it to any significant extent. The earliest example of antithesis in alternate lines that I have been able to find is in a lyric by Su Shih in the meter *Ch'in-yüan Ch'un,* where it occurs in the first stanza but not in the corresponding lines of the second stanza.[60] This appears to be a unique occurence in Su's lyrics. Among lyricists who were Su's contemporaries or juniors but Chou's seniors in age, five wrote lyrics

---

[58] *Ibid.,* p. 602.   [59] *Ibid.,* p. 595.   [60] *Ibid.,* p. 282.

in the meter *Ch'in-yüan Ch'un*.[61] Only one of them, Ch'in Kuan, used antitheses in alternate lines, in both stanzas. Chou himself did not write in this meter; all the instances of this device occur in two other meters, *Feng-liu Tzu* and *Yi-ts'un Chin*,[62] and in each meter it occurs more than once. As far as I know, no one else before Chou used it in these particular meters,[63] so it seems safe to say that what was probably a casual verbal play in Su Shih was consciously imitated by Ch'in Kuan, writing in the same meter, and then applied to other meters and further developed by Chou Pang-yen.

As for the total number of meters used, Chou's one hundred and eighty-six extant and authentic lyrics involve the use of one hundred and fourteen meters, of which thirty-nine are "little airs" and seventy-five "slow lyrics." The shortest of them runs to thirty-three syllables, the longest, one hundred and forty.[64] More than sixty of them were his inventions or new variations on existing meters. All these have been followed by later lyricists and prosodists as standard patterns.

To conclude: although Chou Pang-yen was not as great an innovator as Liu Yung or Su Shih, he made significant contributions to the development of the lyric. He inherited certain themes and styles and brought them to a new culmination. His works are subtle and sophisticated but do not often strike one with immediate force. The poetic worlds of his lyrics are translucent, if not opaque, rather than crystalline, and their verbal structures are like ornately carved ivory or jade rather than simple-shaped porcelain. His influence on later lyricists and critics, especially those of the Ch'ing period (1644–1911), has been immense, even though he is hardly a popular poet among younger Chinese readers today.

[61]Wei Hsiang (1033–1105) in CST, p. 219; Lu Mu (*fl.* 1061), *ibid.*, p. 356; Huang T'ing-chien (1045–1105), *ibid.*, p. 412; Ch'ao Tuan-li (1046–1113), *ibid.*, p. 425; Ch'in Kuan (1049–1100), *ibid.*, p. 455.

[62]*Ibid.*, pp. 595, 604, 614.

[63]The only earlier example of *Feng-liu Tzu* I know of is by Ch'in Kuan (CST, p. 456), and that of *Yi-ts'un Chin* is by Liu Yung (*ibid.*, p. 25). Neither uses antithesis in alternate lines.

[64]The shortest is *Ju-meng Ling*, the longest *Liu-ch'ou*.

CHAPTER 5

Epilogue

In the preceding chapters we have examined the works of six major lyricists of the Northern Sung, both for their intrinsic interests and for the light they might shed on the general trends in the development of the lyric as a poetic genre during this period. We have seen how Yen Shu and Ou-yang Hsiu continued the tradition of the *Hua-chien Anthology* by writing elegant lyrics that embodied refined sentiments and sensibilities; how Liu Yung endowed the lyric with emotional realism and made various stylistic and prosodic innovations, which were imitated by others like Ch'in Kuan; how Su Shih enriched the genre with intellectuality and wit, while extending its thematic scope and stylistic range; and how Chou Pang-yen synthesized earlier styles and achieved new heights of subtlety and sophistication.

In our discussions of these lyricists, we have paid special attention to what seemed distinctive in the works of each, although it has seldom been possible to identify unique qualities or features, in view of the common practice among Chinese poets of imitating their predecessors or contemporaries. Moreover, even if it had been possible, to have confined our attention to each poet's unique qualities would have created a very incomplete impression of his poetry, because some vital elements of poetry, such as imagery, are common to the works of all poets. Thus, although our discussions may have at times appeared *déjà vu,* they have, I hope, shown both the similarities and the differences among the poets discussed, as well as the contributions made by each to the development of the whole genre.

Naturally, not all common poetic features have been fully discussed in the foregoing pages. For instance, alliterative, rhyming, and reduplicative disyllables have been mentioned only in the commentaries on individual poems but not in the discussions of each poet's works as a corpus. It may be of some interest now to see how frequently each poet employed these devices, and then consider their poetic significance in general. In the following table, I shall give the numbers of the three kinds of disyllables found in the lyrics of each of the six poets, as well as the number of occurrences, since some of them occur more than once.

	Yen	Ou-yang	Liu	Ch'in	Su	Chou
Total number of lyrics	132	156*	212	84	302	186
Alliterative disyllables	13	15	21	10	18	15
Occurrences	23	35	30	12	22	29
Rhyming disyllables	13	21	24	9	35	24
Occurrences	15	26	45	9	43	38
Reduplicative disyllables	45	67	94	42	99	66
Occurrences	73	103	254	56	149	97

*This figure does not include the lyrics of questionable authorship.

Although no marked differences among these poets emerge from the above statistics, Liu Yung is seen as the one who made the fullest use of all the devices concerned. His lyrics are therefore particularly rich in auditory effects.

Apart from generally contributing to the auditory effects of lyrics, alliterative, rhyming, and reduplicative disyllables can sometimes specifically reinforce the meaning or the imagery. In addition to the examples we have seen in the lyrics quoted before, a few more may be given here.

The alliterative *ts'en-tz'u* 參差 (Ancient Chinese *ts'iəm-ts'ie*) means "uneven" or "of unequal length," and when applied to bamboos, suggests their jagged appearance; the rhyming disyllables *ch'an-mier* 纏綿 (A.C. *d'iän-miän;* "entangle"), 遷延 *ch'ien-yen* (A.C. *k'ien-iän;* "prolong"), 宛轉 *wan-chuan* (A.C. *·iwɐn-t̯iwän;* "twist and turn"), and 丁寧 *ting-ning* (A.C. *tieng-nieng;* "repeatedly tell") all connote endless repetition or continuation; the reduplicative 去 去 ch'ü-ch'ü (A.C. k'i̯wo-k'i̯wo; "depart, depart") and 迢迢 t'iao-t'iao (A.C. d'ieu-d'ieu; "long, long") naturally emphasize the action or quality described. The effects of onomatopoeic disyllables are even more obvious. For example, hsiao-hsiao 蕭 蕭 (A.C. sieu-sieu) describes the sound of the wind, in a manner similar to the English word "sough."

Many alliterative, rhyming, or reduplicative disyllables are simply the names of common objects, or are common idioms. However, they can still be used to produce auditory or other effects. The disyllable yüan-yang 鴛 鴦 (A.C. ·iwɒn- ·iang), which means "mandarin duck," is a great favorite with several poets, and one suspects that this is not only because the bird denoted by this disyllable has a colorful appearance and a symbolic significance (a pair of mandarin ducks symbolize happy lovers) but also because of the euphony. As for common idioms used for other than auditory effects, an example is jen-jen 人 人 (A.C. ńzi̯ĕn-ńzi̯ĕn; literally "person-person"), which usually means "everyone," but which some lyricists use as an intimate and affectionate way of referring to a woman,[1] as if saying "this very special person." This use of the common expression jen-jen reminds one of Richard Crashaw's use of the pronoun "she" in the lines

Whoe'er she be—
That not impossible She
That shall command my heart and me.[2]

Apart from the six poets discussed, there were many others who wrote fine lyrics, but their works have not been dealt with here, because they seem less representative of general trends or less influential on contemporary and later poets. For example, Chang Hsien (990–1078) is often mentioned in the same breath as Liu Yung, but his lyrics were not as widely known as the latter's in their own lifetimes, and have exerted much less influence on later lyricists. Chang's importance in the history of

---

[1] See CST, pp. 126, 135, 469, 619.
[2] Quiller-Couch, p. 366.

the lyric, therefore, cannot compare with Liu's. Another lyricist much admired by some critics is Yen Chi-tao (1041?–1119?), Yen Shu's youngest son. His lyrics are little influenced by the important innovations Liu Yung and Su Shih effected, and stylistically belong to the tenth century rather than the eleventh.

One lyricist who lived at the end of the Northern Sung period and the beginning of the Southern Sung and whose works therefore fall somewhat outside the temporal scope of this book is the poetess Li Ch'ing-chao (1094–*ca.* 1152).[3] Since she is the most celebrated poetess China has ever produced, she deserves some attention. Her lyrics deal with the familiar themes of love, sorrow, nostalgia, and solitude, but she explores them with particularly keen sensibility and unusual emotional depth. Technically, her greatest achievements lie in her daring use of common but unexpected words (such as *lu fei hung shou,*綠肥紅瘦 "green fat, red thin," meaning that the green foliage has grown luxuriant and the red flowers have faded; and *ch'ung liu chiao hua,* 寵柳嬌花 "favored willows, pampered flowers"), and her consummate skill in manipulating auditory effects. Her most famous line is a unique example of seven reduplicative disyllabic compounds: *hsün-hsün mi-mi leng-leng ch'ing-ch'ing ch'i-ch'i ts'an-ts'an ch'i-ch'i*[4] 尋尋覓覓冷冷清清悽悽慘慘戚戚 (A.C.: *ziəm-ziəm, miek-miek, lɒng-lɒng, tsʻiäng-tsʻiäng, tsʻiei-tsʻiei, tsʻậm-tsʻậm, tsʻiek-tsʻiek*), meaning literally "seek-seek, search-search, cold-cold, quiet-quiet, sad-sad, sorrowful-sorrowful, grieved-grieved." These disyllabic compounds, with their reiterated short vowels and aspirate affricates, intensify the feelings of coldness and agitation by suggesting shivering and clenched teeth. Naturally much of the effect is lost in translation.[5]

Being a virtuoso herself, Li Ch'ing-chao made some caustic re-

[3]Li Ch'ing-chao's dates are given according to Huang Sheng-chang, pp. 117–63. There is a biography of Li in English, but it is neither up-to-date in scholarship nor mature in critical judgment. There is also an article in English on her poetry by K. Y. Hsu.

[4]Li Ch'ing-chao, p. 31; CST, p. 932.

[5]Translations of this lyric include those by Teresa Li in Ch'en Shou-yi, p. 406; Liu Wu-chi, p. 117; Ayling and Mackintosh, p. 147.

marks about practically all her predecessors in the lyric genre. She said of Liu Yung's lyrics: "they agree with the music but their words are vulgar and low"; of the lyrics of Yen Shu, Ou-yang Hsiu, and Su Shih: "they are only poems [*shih*] in lines of uneven length [and not real *lyrics*] and often disagree with the music"; and of Ch'in Kuan's lyric poetry: "it is like a beautiful girl from a poor family—even if she is extremely attractive and graceful, she lacks an air of nobility and aristocracy after all."[6] Actually her own lyrics are not free from the influences of some of the poets she so harshly criticized. For instance, she took Ou-yang's line "Deep deep lies the courtyard—who knows how deep?" (No. 8 in this book) and incorporated it in several lyrics.[7] In another lyric, she borrowed Liu Yung's line "the coverlet tosses its red waves" (see above, p. 84), although she gave it an ironic twist: in Liu's lyric, the image describes two lovers in bed, in Li's it refers to the speaker tossing sleepless in bed alone.[8] Even her famous line "green fat, red thin" is reminiscent of Liu's "green sad, red grieving" (*lu ts'an hung ch'ou* 綠慘紅愁).[9]

Both in her technical virtuosity and in her highly critical attitude towards other poets, Li Ch'ing-chao resembles Edith Sitwell; and just as Sitwell can hardly be said to have the same stature as Yeats or Eliot, so Li Ch'ing-chao can hardly be said to have the same stature as Liu Yung or Su Shih.

The subsequent development of the lyric during the Southern Sung period will be sketched below. Broadly speaking, we may discern two main tendencies. On the one hand, some lyricists, influenced by Su Shih and shocked by the occupation of North China by the Juchen Tartars, used the lyric to express heroic, patriotic sentiments or philosophical attitudes towards life, generally in an erudite style. On the other hand, lyricists who followed Chou Pang-yen escaped into their own private worlds of

----

[6]Li Ch'ing-chao, p. 79. For discussions of her views on lyric poetry, see Teng K'uei-ying, Huang Mo-ku.

[7]CST, pp. 929, 933; Li Ch'ing-chao, pp. 18–19.

[8]CST, p. 928; Li Ch'ing-chao, p. 29.

[9]CST, p. 25.

intimate feeling and aesthetic experience and developed extremely oblique and often ambiguous modes of expression.

The greatest of the heroic-philosphical lyricists of the period is Hsin Ch'i-chi (1140–1207), of whom an admirable study in English has recently been written by Irving Lo.[10] The most prolific of all Sung lyricists (his surviving lyrics number six hundred and twenty-six), Hsin wrote on all kinds of subjects and varied his style accordingly, but his most representative lyrics are those which give vent to his frustrated ambitions to help recover North China from the invaders, or reflect his calmer moods of quiet enjoyment of Nature and stoic resignation to his lot in life. His typical style is powerful and free, marked by the ubiquitous presence of allusions, quotations, and derivations, frequent uses of prose particles and prose syntax, and relative scarcity of imagery. Most of these features he inherited from Su Shih, but he carried them perilously close to excesses. Indeed, though Hsin himself was able to mould his literary sources into new poetic shapes, his imitators, who lacked his breadth of vision and imaginative power, all too often lapsed into pedantry and flatness.

Among the followers of Chou Pang-yen, the most important one is Chiang K'uei (*ca.* 1155 to *ca.* 1221).[11] An expert in music, he not only wrote lyrics to existing tunes, but also, contrary to common practice, composed tunes to fit the words he had written first. Yet he was no mere craftsman concerned only with musical and prosodic niceties but a genuine poet who happened to be a composer as well.

As a poet, Chiang is even more subtle and sophisticated than his predecessor Chou Pang-yen, and his poetic worlds are often rarefied and remote from everyday existence. He eschews strong emotion but contemplates life in a cool and calm manner, albeit with a tinge of sadness at times. When he recalls a love affair, there is no suggestion of erotic passion, not even remembered passion, but only lingering memories of beauty loved and lost;

[10] Irving Yucheng Lo, *passim.* For annotated edition of Hsin, see Teng Kuang-ming.

[11] See Hsia Ch'eng-t'ao, II. There is another annotated edition by Lai Ch'iao-pen.

when he laments the devastations of war, there are no patriotic outbursts, but only subdued sighs. Even such restrained but relatively explicit expressions are not typical of his manner; usually he would reveal some emotional or aesthetic experience through imagery and literary allusions. Many of his lyrics ostensibly describe such objects as plum blossoms or chirping crickets, and later critics have inevitably interpreted these allegorically. However, although some of them may involve political or personal allegory, it is doubtful if an allegorical interpretation is valid for all. It would seem more profitable to read such lyrics symbolically, recognizing deeper meanings than the literal, but not attempting to identify elements in a poem with actual persons or events.[12]

The last lyricist I shall discuss is Wu Wen-ying (*ca.* 1200 to *ca.* 1260),[13] who has been harshly condemned by some critics for his alleged obscurity, triviality, and incoherence, but extravagantly praised by others who see in his lyrics great subtlety, complexity, and profundity. While the adverse criticisms are probably due to failure to perceive the underlying structures of his works, the ecstatic acclaims generally overlook the fact that his lyrics are confined to a very narrow range of human experience and reveal an inward-turning, self-centered consciousness. Only a handful of his lyrics show a sense of history and may possibly lament the fall of the Sung (in highly ambiguous and oblique terms); the rest are concerned with recollections of past love affairs, social occasions such as farewell parties and birthdays, and descriptions of natural objects, particularly flowers. In contrast to Chiang K'uei, Wu Wen-ying revels in passion, which, although never explicitly described, is yet intense in its self-torment and persistence. However, his constant complaints of loneliness, aging, and illness create pathos, if not bathos, rather than tragedy. As for the lyrics describing natural objects, some may contain personal allegory alluding to a former concubine or a deceased courtesan, but others are merely ingenious verbal miniature paintings.

[12] For an analysis of one of Chiang K'uei's lyrics, see J. J. Y. Liu, III.

[13] For Wu Wen-ying's dates, see Hsia Ch'eng-t'ao, III, pp. 457–80. For annotated editions of Wu's lyrics, see Yang T'ieh-fu, Huang Shao-fu.

Wu's use of language is more remarkable than his exploration of reality. Nonetheless, the claims of originality made on his behalf by a recent writer are rather exaggerated.[14] It is true that Wu often uses striking and farfetched imagery, is fond of fusing past and present, and relies on emotional associations instead of logical connections for the structural unity of his lyrics; but he was by no means the first to do any of these things. In the present book alone we have encountered numerous instances of farfetched imagery and of the fusion of past and present. As for the associational technique, this is as old as Chinese poetry itself, being one of the three main modes of expression of the *Book of Poetry*, known as *hsing* (literally "arousal").[15] Furthermore, Wu is certainly not free from clichés. To give just one example, he alludes to the mythical lady in the moon, Ch'ang-o, as a substitute for "moon," no less than fifteen times in his lyrics. In sum, though some of Wu's lyrics exhibit incredibly complex structures and are rich in emotional and sensuous appeals, his poetry as a whole can best be described as "rococo," because of its extravagant ornamentation, fantastic flights of fancy, and preoccupation with minute details, with concommitant lack of robustness, grandeur, and sublimity.

By the end of the Southern Sung period (1279), the lyric had lost much of its creative vitality, although it had remained a popular poetic medium. Since then, many have written poetry in lyric meters, but few have been able to equal, let alone surpass, the achievements of the Sung lyricists in their explorations of reality and of the Chinese language.

[14]Chia-ying Yeh Chao, pp. 53-59.

[15]This is of course an oversimplified interpretation of *hsing*. For a full discussion see Shih-hsiang Ch'en.

BIBLIOGRAPHY

This is not a comprehensive bibliography of Sung *tz'u* but only a list of works cited or referred to in the present book. I have been criticized for listing only such works, but I see no point in including works that I found neither useful nor stimulating.

Abbreviations:

CKWH = *Chung-kuo wen-hsüeh chen-pen ts'ung-shu* 中國文學珍本叢書, Shanghai.

CL = *Chinese Literature*, Peking.

CST = *Ch'üan Sung tz'u.* See T'ang Kuei-chang, V.

CTS = *Ch'üan T'ang shih* 全唐詩, preface 1707; page numbers refer to the Peking, 1960 edition.

HJAS = *Harvard Journal of Asiatic Studies.*

SPPY = *Ssu-pu pei-yao* 四部備要, Shanghai, 1927–1935.

SS = *Sung shih* 宋史 (Po-na edition).

STKW = *(Taiwan sheng-li) Shih-fan Ta-hsüeh kuo-wen yen-chiu-so chi-k'an* 台灣省立師範大學國文研究所集刊.

TF = *Tz'u fan.* See Yen Pin-tu.

THTP = *Tz'u-hua ts'ung-pien.* See T'ang Kuei-chang, I.

TL = *Tz'u lü.* See Wan Shu.

TP = *(Ch'in-ting) Tz'u p'u.* See Wang Yi-ch'ing, II.

TSTY = *T'ang Sung tz'u yen-chiu lun-wen chi* 唐宋詞研究論文集, Hong Kong, 1969.

WHYC = *Wen-hsüeh yi-ch'an tseng-k'an* 文學遺產增刊, Peking.

Anon., *(Hsin-k'an) Ta Sung Hsüan-ho yi-shih* 新刊大宋宣和遺事, (13th c.), rep. Shanghai, 1954.

Ayling, Alan, and Duncan Mackintosh, *A Collection of Chinese Lyrics,* London, 1956.

Baxter, Glen William, "Metrical Origins of the *Tz'u,*" HJAS, Vol. 16, 1953; rep. in John L. Bishop, ed., *Studies in Chinese Literature,* Cambridge, Mass., 1966.

Birch, Cyril, ed., I, *Anthology of Chinese Literature,* New York, 1965.

——, ed., II, *Studies in Chinese Literary Genres,* Berkeley, 1973.

Chang Hui-yen 張惠言 (1761–1802), *Tz'u hsüan* 詞選, preface 1797.

Chang Wan 張婉 (pseudonym), *P'u-sa-man chi-ch'i hsiang-kuan chih chu wen-t'i* 菩薩蠻及其相關之諸問題, *Ta-lu tsa-chih* 大陸雜誌, Vol. 20, Nos. 1–3, 1960.

Chao, Chia-ying Yeh, "Wu Wen-ying's *Tz'u*: a Modern View," HJAS, Vol. 29, 1969.

Ch'en Shih-ch'üan, "The Rise of the *Tz'u,* Reconsidered," *Journal of the American Oriental Society,* Vol. 90, No. 2, 1970.

Ch'en Shih-hsiang, "The *Shih Ching*: Its Generic Significance in Chinese Literary History and Poetics," in Birch, ed., II.

Ch'en Shou-yi, *Chinese Literature, a Historical Introduction,* New York, 1961.

Ch'en T'ing-cho 陳廷焯 (1853–1892), *Pai-yü-chai tz'u-hua* 白雨齋詞話, in THTP.

Ch'en Yüan-lung 陳元龍 (early 13th c.), ed., *P'ien-yü tz'u* 片玉詞, in SPPY.

Cheng Ch'ien 鄭騫, I, *Tz'u hsüan* 詞選, Taipei, 1952; 2nd impression, 1953.

——, II, *Ts'ung shih tao ch'ü* 從詩到曲, Taipei, 1961.

Chiang Chao-lan 蔣兆蘭, *Tz'u shuo* 詞說, in THTP.

Chiang Shang-hsien 姜尚賢, I, *Sung ssu-ta-chia tz'u yen-chiu* 宋四大家詞研究, Tainan, 1962.

——, II, *T'ang Sung ming-chia tz'u hsin-hsüan* 唐宋名家詞新選, Tainan, 1963.

Chin Jen-jui 金人瑞 (d. 1661), *Ch'ang-ching-t'ang ts'ai-tzu-shu hui-pien* 唱經堂才子書彙編, in CKWH, 1935.

Ch'in Kuan 秦 觀 (1049-1100). For editions used, see CST, Mao Chin, Jao Tsung-yi, II. There is also an annotated ed. by Hsü Wen-chu.

Chou Chi 周 濟 (1781-1839), I, *Sung ssu-chia tz'u hsüan* 宋四家詞選, preface 1832, rep. Hong Kong, 1959.

———, II, *Chieh-ts'un-chai lun-tz'u tsa-chu* 介存齋論詞雜著 in THTP.

Chou Fa-kao 周法高, *Chung-kuo ku-tai yü-fa, kou-tz'u pien* 中國古代語法 構詞編, Taipei, 1962.

Chou Pang-yen 周邦彥 (1056-1121). For editions used, see CST, Ch'en Yüan-lung, Yang Yi-lin.

Chu Tsu-mou 朱祖謀 (1857-1931), ed., I, *Ch'iang-ts'un ts'ung-shu* 彊村叢書, Shanghai, 1922.

———, ed., II, *Sung tz'u san-pai-shou.* See T'ang Kuei-chang, IV.

Chu Yi-tsun 朱彝尊 (1629-1709), *Tz'u tsung* 詞綜, in SPPY.

Downer, G. B., and A. C. Graham, "Tone Patterns in Chinese Poetry," *Bulletin of the School of Oriental and African Studies,* London, Vol. XXVI, Part 1, 1963.

Feng Chi-wu 馮集梧, ed., *Fan-ch'uan shih-chi chu* 樊川詩集注, preface 1798, in SPPY.

Feng Ch'i-yung 馮其庸, "*Lun Pei-Sung ch'ien-ch'i liang-chung pu-t'ung-te tz'u-feng*" 論北宋前期兩種不同的詞風, WHYC, 8th series, 1961; rep. in TSTY.

Feng Hao 馮浩 (1719-1801), ed., *Yü-hsi-sheng shih chien-chu* 玉溪生詩箋注, 1780, in SPPY.

Fisher-Jorgensen, Eli, "New Techniques of Acoustic Phonetics," in Sol Saporta, ed., *Psycholinguistics,* New York, 1961.

Gernet, Jacques (Tr. H. M. Wright), *Daily Life in China on the Eve of the Mongol Invasion,* London, 1962.

Housman, A. E. (1859-1936), *Complete Poems,* New York, 1959.

Hsia Ch'eng-t'ao 夏承燾, I, *T'ang Sung tz'u lun-ts'ung* 唐宋詞論叢, Shanghai, 1956; 3rd impression, 1958.

———, ed., II, *Chiang Pai-shih tz'u pien-nien chien-chiao* 姜白石詞編年箋校, Shanghai, 1958; 2nd impression, 1961.

———, III, *T'ang Sung tz'u-jen nien-p'u* 唐宋詞人年譜, new ed., Shanghai, 1961.

——— and Sheng T'ao-ch'ing 盛弢青, eds., *T'ang Sung tz'u hsüan* 唐宋詞選, Peking, 1962.

Hsü Fu-kuan 徐復觀, *Chung-kuo wen-hsüeh lun-chi* 中國文學論集, Taichung, 1966.

Hsu, K. Y., "The Poems of Li Ch'ing-chao," *Publications of the Modern Language Association,* Vol. LXXVII, No. 5, 1962.

Hsü Wen-chu 徐文助, ed., *Huai-hai shih chu fu tz'u chiao-chu* 淮海詩注附詞校注, STKW, No. 12, 1968.

Hsüeh Li-jo 薛礪若, *Sung tz'u t'ung-lun* 宋詞通論, Shanghai, 1937; rep. Taipei, 1958.

Hu Yün-yi 胡雲翼, *Sung tz'u hsüan* 宋詞選, Shanghai, 1962; 4th impression, 1965.

Huang Mo-ku 黃墨谷, "*Tui Li Ch'ing-chao tz'u pieh shih yi-chia shuo te li-chieh*" 對李清照詞別是一家說的理解, WHYC, 12th series, 1963; rep. in TSTY.

Huang Shao-fu 黃少甫, ed., *Meng-ch'uang tz'u chiao-ting chien-chu* 夢窗詞校訂箋注, STKW, No. 10, 1966.

Huang Sheng-chang 黃盛璋, *Chao Ming-ch'eng Li Ch'ing-chao fu-fu nien-p'u* 趙明誠李清照夫婦年譜, in Li Ch'ing-chao.

Jao Tsung-yi 饒宗頤, I, *Tz'u chi k'ao* 詞籍考, Hong Kong, 1963.

———, ed., II, *Ying Sung Ch'ien-tao Kao-yu-chün-hsüeh pen Huai-hai-chü-shih ch'ang-tuan-chü* 景宋乾道高郵軍學本淮海居士長短句, Hong Kong, 1965.

Jakobson, Roman, "The Modular Design of Chinese Regulated Verse," in J. Pouillon and P. Maranda, eds., *Échanges et Communications, Mélanges offerts à Claude Lévi-Strauss,* The Hague, 1970.

Karlgren, Bernhard, *Grammata Serica Recensa,* Stockholm, 1957.

Lai Ch'iao-pen 賴橋本, ed., *Pai-shih tz'u chien-chiao chi yen-chiu* 白石詞箋校及研究, STKW, No. 11, 1967.

Li Ch'ing-chao 李清照 (1084 to ca. 1152), *Li-Ch'ing-chao chi* 李清照集, Shanghai, 1962.

Li Shang-yin 李商隱 (813–858). See Feng Hao.

Li Yü 李煜 (937–978). See Wang Tz'u-ts'ung.

Liang Ch'i-hsün 梁啟勳 , Tz'u hsüeh ch'üan-heng 詞學詮衡 , Hong Kong, 1964.

Lin Yutang, *The Gay Genius,* New York, 1947.

Liu, James J. Y., I, *The Art of Chinese Poetry,* London and Chicago, 1962; Phoenix Books ed., Chicago, 1966; 3rd impression, 1970.

——, II, *The Poetry of Li Shang-yin,* Chicago, 1969.

——, III, "Some Literary Qualities of the Lyric," in Birch, ed., II.

Liu, James T. C., *Ou-yang Hsiu,* Stanford, 1967.

Liu Ta-chieh 劉大杰 , *Chung-kuo wen-hsüeh fa-chan shih* 中國文學發展史 , Shanghai, 1957.

Liu Wu-chi, *An Introduction to Chinese Literature,* Bloomington, Indiana, 1966.

Liu Yü-hsi 劉禹錫 (772–842), *Liu Pin-k'e chi* 劉賓客集 , in SPPY.

Lo, Irving Yucheng, *Hsin Ch'i-chi,* New York, 1971.

Lu K'an-ju 陸侃如 and Feng Yüan-chün 馮沅君 , *Chung-kuo shih-shih* 中國詩史 , Rev. ed., Peking, 1956.

Lung Yü-sheng 龍榆生 (Lung Mu-hsün 龍沐勛), ed., *Tung-p'o yüeh-fu chien* 東坡樂府箋 , Shanghai, 1936; 2nd ed., 1958

Mao Chin 毛晉 (1598–1659), *Sung liu-shih ming-chia tz'u* 宋六十名家詞 , rep. in CKWH, 1936.

Marlowe, Christopher, *The Tragical History of Doctor Faustus* (ed., F. S. Boas), London, 1949.

Mei Tsu-lin, "Tones and Prosody in Middle Chinese and the Origins of the Rising Tone," HJAS, Vol. 30, 1970.

Meng Ch'i 孟棨 (T'ang period), *Pen-shih shih* 本事詩 , in Ting Fu-pao.

Meng Chiao 孟郊 (751–814), *Meng Tung-yeh chi* 孟東野集 , in SPPY.

Meng Yüan-lao 孟元老 , *Tung-ching meng-hua-lu* 東京夢華錄 , 1147; with notes by Teng Chih-ch'eng 鄧之誠 , rep. Taipei, 1963.

Ou-yang Hsiu 歐陽修 (1007–1072). For editions consulted, see CST, Jao Tsung-yi, II, and note 47 to Ch. 1.

Payne, Robert, ed., *The White Pony,* New York, 1947; Mentor Book ed., 1960.

Pian, Rulan Chao, *Sonq [Sung] Dynasty Musical Sources and Their Interpretation,* Cambridge, Mass., 1967.

Po Chü-yi 白居易 (772–846), *Po Hsiang-shan shih-chi* 白香山詩集, in SPPY.

Quiller-Couch, Sir Arthur, ed., *The Oxford Book of English Verse,* Oxford, 1939; rep. 1948.

Shen Hsiung 沈雄, *Ku-chin tz'u-hua* 古今詞話, 1689, rep. in THTP.

Su Shih 蘇軾 (1037–1101). For editions used, see CST, Lung Yü-sheng.

T'an Wei 譚蔚, *T'ang Sung tz'u pai-shou ch'ien-shih* 唐宋詞百首淺釋, Changsha, 1958.

Tanaka Kenji 田中謙二, *Ōyō Shu no shi ni tsuite* 歐陽修の詞について, *Tōhō Gaku* 東方學, No. 7, 1953.

T'ang Kuei-chang 唐圭璋, I, ed., *Tz'u-hua ts'ung-pien* 詞話叢編, Nanking, 1935; rep. Taipei, 1967.

——, II, "*Liu Yung shih-chi hsin-cheng*" 柳永事迹新証, *Wen-hsüeh yen-chiu* 文學研究, Peking, 1957, No. 3.

——, III, *Sung tz'u ssu-k'ao* 宋詞四考, Nanking, 1959.

——, IV, ed., *Sung tz'u san-pai-shou chien-chu* 宋詞三百首箋注, preface 1957; rep. Hong Kong, 1961.

——, V, ed., *Ch'üan Sung tz'u* 全宋詞, new ed., Shanghai, 1965.

Tay, C. N., "From *Snow* to *Plum Blossoms*," *Journal of Asian Studies,* Vol. XXV, No. 2, 1966.

Teng Kuang-ming 鄧廣銘, ed., *Chia-hsüan tz'u pien-nien chien-chu* 稼軒詞編年箋注, new ed., Shanghai, 1962.

Teng K'uei-ying 鄧魁英, "*Kuan-yü Li Ch'ing-chao tz'u-lun te p'ing-chia wen-t'i*" 關於李清照詞論的評價問題, WHYC, 12th series, 1963; rep. in TSTY.

Ting Fu-pao 丁福保, ed., *Li-tai shih-hua hsü-pien* 歷代詩話續編, 1915; rep. Taipei, no date, under the name of Ting Chung-hu 丁仲祜.

Ting Shao-yi 丁紹儀, *T'ing-ch'iu-sheng-kuan tz'u-hua* 聽秋聲館詞話, 1869, rep. in THTP.

Ting Sheng-shu 丁聲樹, *Ku-chin tzu-yin tui-chao shou-ts'e* 古今字音對照手冊, Peking, 1958.

Ts'ai Te-an 蔡德安, *Tz'u-hsüeh hsin-lun* 詞學新論, Taipei, 1963.

Tu Fu 杜甫 (712–770), *Concordance*. Harvard-Yenching Sinological Index Series, Supplement 14, rep. Taipei, 1966.

Tu Mu 杜牧 (803–852). See Feng Chi-wu.

T'u Ching-i, tr., *Poetic Remarks in the Human World* (translation of Wang Kuo-wei, I), Taipei, 1970.

Wan Min-hao 宛敏灝, *Erh Yen chi-ch'i tz'u* 二晏及其詞, Shanghai, 1934.

Wan Shu 萬樹, *Tz'u lü* 詞律, preface 1687, rep. with supplements by Hsü Pen-li 徐本立 and Tu Wen-lan 杜文瀾, in SPPY.

Wang Kuo-wei 王國維 (1877–1927), I, *Jen-chien tz'u-hua* 人間詞話, in THTP.

——, II, *Ch'ing-chen hsien-sheng yi-shih* 清真先生遺事, in *Hai-ning Wang Ching-an hsien-sheng yi-shu* 海寧王靜安先生遺書, Changsha, 1940.

Wang Li 王力, *Han-yü shih-lü hsüeh* 漢語詩律學, Shanghai, 1958.

Wang Tz'u-ts'ung 王次聰, ed., *Nan T'ang erh-chu tz'u chiao-chu* 南唐二主詞校注, Taipei, no date

Wang Yi-ch'ing 王奕清 et al., eds., I, *(Yü-hsüan) Li-tai shih-yü* 御選歷代詩餘, 1707; *chüan* 111–120 rep. in THTP.

——, eds., II, *(Ch'in-ting) Tz'u-p'u* 欽定詞譜, 1715; rep. Taipei, 1964.

Watson, Burton, *Su Tung-p'o, Selections from a Sung Dynasty Poet*, New York, 1965.

Wei Chuang 韋莊 (836?–910), *Wei Chuang chi* 韋莊集, Peking, 1958.

Wellek, René, and Austin Warren, *Theory of Literature*, 3rd ed., New York, 1962.

Wen Ju-hsien 聞汝賢, *Tz'u-p'ai hui-shih* 詞牌彙釋, Taipei, 1963.

Wu Shih-tao 吳師道 (14th c.), *Wu Li-pu tz'u-hua* 吳禮部詞話, in THTP.

Yang Hsien-yi   楊憲益,   *Ling-mo hsin-chien*   零墨新箋, Shanghai, 1947.

Yang Shen 楊慎 (1488–1559), *Tz'u-p'in* 詞品, in THTP.

Yang T'ieh-fu 楊鐵夫, ed., *Kai-cheng Meng-ch'uang tz'u chien-shih* 改正夢窗詞箋 釋, 2nd ed., Shanghai, 1933.

Yang Yi-lin 楊易霖, ed., *Chou tz'u ting-lü* 周詞定律, 1935; rep. Hong Kong, 1963.

Yen K'e-chün 嚴可均 (1762–1843), ed., *Ch'üan Shang-ku San-tai Ch'in Han San-kuo Liu-ch'ao wen* 全上古三代秦 漢三國六朝文, rep. Shanghai, 1958.

Yen Pin-tu 嚴賓杜, *Tz'u fan* 詞範, Taipei, 1959.

Yen Shu 晏殊 (991–1055). For editions consulted, see CST, Jao Tsung-yi, II.

Yoshikawa Kōjiro 吉川幸次郎, I (Tr. B. Watson), *An Introduction to Sung Poetry*, Cambridge, Mass., 1967.

———, II, *Yoshikawa Kōjiro zen-shu* 吉川幸次郎全集, Vol. 13, Tokyo, 1969.

Yü P'ing-po 俞平伯, *Ch'ing-chen-tz'u shih* 清真詞釋, Shanghai, 1949.

Library of Congress Cataloging in Publication Data

Liu, James J Y
    Major lyricists of the Northern Sung (A.D. 960-1126).

    Includes lyrics in English and Chinese.
    Bibliography: p.
    1. Tz'u—History and criticism.   I.   Title.
PL2343.L5   895.1'1'04   73-10290
ISBN 0-691-06259-5